BORDER CROSSING:
FILM IN IRELAND, BRITAIN AND EUROPE

BORDER CROSSING:
FILM IN IRELAND, BRITAIN AND EUROPE

EDITED BY JOHN HILL, MARTIN McLOONE and PAUL HAINSWORTH

Institute of Irish Studies in association with the University of Ulster and the British Film Institute

Published 1994
The Institute of Irish Studies
The Queen's University of Belfast
in association with the University of Ulster
and the British Film Institute

Grateful acknowledgement for financial assistance is made to the
Cultural Traditions Group of the Community Relations Council and
the University of Ulster.

ISBN 0 85 170 4891 X
ISBN 0 85 389 504 X

British Library Cataloguing-in-Publication Data. A catalogue record for this
book is available from the British Library.

Printed by W&G Baird Ltd., Antrim
Cover design by Rodney Miller Associates

CONTENTS

ACKNOWLEDGEMENTS

The editors would like to thank Mervyn McKay for all his help with the preparation of this book. Thanks also to Janetta Chambers, Gillian Coward, and Willie Norris.

INTRODUCTION

John Hill

As this book was being finalised, the issue of the European film industry unexpectedly hit the headlines. This was the result of the talks surrounding GATT (the General Agreement on Tariffs and Trade) which were finally concluded, after seven years, on 15 December 1993. The agreement, however, was in jeopardy until almost the last moment. Surprisingly, the main reason for this was a dispute between the United States and Europe (especially France) over the film and television industries. It was a dispute which had been brewing for some time and revolved around the various measures which the European countries employed in support of the audio-visual industries, such as television quotas, co-production treaties and both national and pan-European film funds.[1] The Americans sought the abolition of all European quotas and subsidies on the grounds that they distorted free trade while the Europeans wished to exempt the audio-visual industries from the GATT agreement on the grounds that European films and television programmes were not simply a matter of 'trade' but were also activities of cultural importance. The week before a final agreement was reached the American negotiators, led by Mickey Kantor, appeared to have agreed to allow the European Union (formerly Community) to maintain its quotas and subsidies but were holding out for a share for US film-makers of the proceeds from levies on cinema tickets, video rentals and sales of blank video cassettes.[2] However, even this demand had to be put aside when, in order to settle the overall trade deal, the US and European negotiators 'agreed to disagree' on the matter of the audio-visual industries. The audio-visual sector will still be bound by the general rules for trade laid down by the agreement but, according to the European negotiators, 'Europe will be able to follow the audio-visual policy it wants'.[3]

The GATT negotiations, therefore, provide this book with a fitting context as it is the future of audio-visual policy in Europe, especially in relation to film, with which it is concerned. The reason this has become such an issue, and why it was so hotly contested during the GATT round, is, of course, because the European cinema is in decline. As John Hill's chapter in this volume demonstrates, the number of European films being made, the size of their audience and their share of the European film and video market are all falling. In contrast, the US share of the EC market rose steadily during the 1980s, reaching over 77 per cent by 1990. Indeed, given the extent of the United States share of the European market, and also the imbalance of trade between the US and Europe which results, it is difficult to understand quite why the Americans pursued the issue of film, during the GATT negotiations, with such extraordinary vigour.[4]

Hollywood's domination of European markets is not, of course, a new phenomenon and stretches back to at least the end of World War One. What is new, however, is the extent of the domination and, in an age of television, video and satellite, the way that this has undermined the viability of even the largest of European film industries. As Martin McLoone suggests, citing the Cuban film-maker and theorist Julio Garcia Espinosa, once successful European film industries are now experiencing the sort of problems which most Third World countries have always faced. However, as McLoone goes on to argue in his chapter, the history of European cinema has itself been uneven and certain of the smaller European countries have also never enjoyed the kind of industry or cinema which was characteristic of their larger European neighbours. As such, it may now be the experience of those very countries, where film-making has always been a struggle, which can most usefully inform the larger debates surrounding the future of European cinema.

It is in this sense that the origins of this book have a relevance to what follows. The book developed out of a film event in March 1993 on the University of Ulster's Jordanstown campus in Belfast. Partly sponsored by the Northern Ireland Film Council, it was called 'Cinema and Europe: Diversity and Identity' and sought, among other things, to bring together film professionals, academics and critics (many of whom appear in this volume) to discuss Irish film in the context of Europe. As Kevin Rockett indicates in his essay below, the Republic of Ireland, with one of the smallest populations in Europe, has experienced a chequered history of film production. Northern Ireland, as Geraldine Wilkins points out, has fared even worse, given its geographical location on the periphery of the UK and its marginal significance to what is conventionally described as the 'British' film industry. The questions which film-making in Ireland, north and south, then give rise to are both economic and cultural: questions concerning not only the economic basis on which film production can proceed in these areas but also the cultural importance of such activity taking place. Ireland has held a special place in the cinematic imagination but its representation in film has, until relatively recently, been left to the British and American cinemas. In recent years, Northern Ireland, as a result of the 'troubles', has also provided the inspiration for a number of features but these too have rarely been homegrown. The Irish situation, in this respect, is analogous to that of Scotland which, as a small nation within the UK, has faced many of the same economic problems as Ireland in sustaining a film industry. It is also a country, whose location on the 'celtic' periphery, has meant that many of its most enduring cinematic representations have been the work of outsiders. Both the economic and cultural dilemmas which this situation gives rise to are diagnosed by Steve McIntyre and Colin McArthur in their contributions. McIntyre provides a realistic assessment of the prospects for film-making in Scotland while McArthur argues for the necessity of films which grapple with the very complexities and contradictions of the nation which the dominant cinematic representations of Scotland either smooth out or omit altogether.

However, if the Irish and Scottish film industries have confronted a common situation as the 'poor relations' of Europe, their predicament is now shared with film industries across Europe as they are forced to face up to Hollywood's increased global dominance. Thus, the British (or, to be strictly accurate, English) film industry, which, if never robust, could at least sustain a reasonably popular national cinema up until the 1970s, is now having to adjust to the situation of insecurity and marginality which has always been the lot of the Irish industry. In doing so, the British and other larger European industries, such as those of France and Italy, have also had to engage more fully with those economic and cultural debates which have characteristically been associated with film-making in the smaller countries. At an economic level, such debates revolve around what are the most appropriate economic strategies for the European industries to follow. David Puttnam, drawing in part on his own experience as a producer, argues in his chapter that it is in the area of big-budget film-making that Europe is weakest and certainly there is considerable support across Europe for encouraging the emergence of a big-budget cinema which will match that of Hollywood. Such a strategy, it is argued, may not be feasible for any single European industry but should be possible if individual industries combine resources. Other contributors to this book are less sure. Steve McIntyre provides a telling analysis of the economic reasons for Hollywood's global dominance and sees little prospect of Europe overturning this competitive advantage. John Hill is equally sceptical about demands for a big-budget pan-European cinema. Indeed, what emerges as something of a consensus amongst many of the writers in this book is support for the view that Europe would be best served by the adoption of a low-budget strategy. It is only this strategy, it is argued, that can lay the basis for a stable and ongoing industry and avoid the vulnerability to huge losses which big-budget film-making involves. However, support for a low-budget cinema does not rest upon economic arguments alone. For, as various contributors argue, it can also have benefits for the films which are then made: their makers suffer from less interference, there is less necessity to pander to what is imagined to be international tastes and there is also enhanced scope for addressing the specificities of the cultures from which they emerge.

In a sense it is these larger cultural questions which the decline of European cinema has brought to the forefront. Indeed, one of the ironies of the GATT talks, supposedly about 'trade', was how in the end they pivoted upon questions of culture. This resort to cultural arguments in order to secure special treatment for the European audio-visual industry has also helped to clarify the objectives of European audio-visual policy and make it apparent that projects such as the European Union's MEDIA programme are cultural in character and not, as some would have it, purely commercial. However, if cultural arguments can now be seen to be of central importance to European audio-visual policy, they must also be treated with some caution. For what often underpinned the appeal to culture in the GATT talks was a relatively simplistic opposition betweeen 'American' culture on the one hand and

'European' culture on the other. Both terms, however, are not so straightforward. The idea of Hollywood films as simply and unproblematically American, for example, does not survive close inspection. As Philip French so vividly demonstrates, while Hollywood may have successfully provided the US with some of its most potent myths it was nonetheless the creation of – mostly European – outsiders and has continued to act as a magnet for European film-makers up until the present day. Moreover, Hollywood films have now been so massively present in Europe and have provided such a stimulus to the creativity of Europeans, including film-makers, that it is difficult to conceive of Hollywood cinema as particularly 'other'. Indeed, European audiences figure increasingly in Hollywood's calculations and it may be helpful to think of Hollywood less as a national cinema than a global one, which Europeans have not only helped to create but which they have also, at least in part, integrated into their own culture. However, while Hollywood may have succeeded in establishing a global standard of film-making this has not then eliminated the need for indigeneous film cultures which serve the local viewpoint. As Martin McLoone argues quite strongly, it is precisely because Hollywood increasingly speaks with a globalising voice that competing voices, rooted in local cultures, have become that much more important and necessary.

However, just as the idea of a straightforwardly homogeneous American culture must be treated with some suspicion so must any idea of a unified European culture. Thus, in seeking to fend off the threat of Europe's 'Americanisation', it has been common practice to appeal to the idea of a shared European culture as an emblem of what is being subject to attack. However, the idea of one shared European culture is a problematic one and Paul Hainsworth's overview of European cultural policy brings out many of the conflicting definitions and 'imaginings' of European identity and culture which have surfaced, particularly in relation to the European Community (now Union). Indeed, it is almost axiomatic for many of the contributions to this book that identities and cultures are generally polyglot in character, liable to change and the source of competing versions of community. This is then the reason why a number of contributors express suspicion towards the idea of a 'European' film policy which seeks to build a 'European' cinema out of assumed common European materials (although Philip French does make a convincing case for certain

films which successfully work with what might otherwise be
regarded as the standard ingredients of the 'Euro-pudding').
However, as McLoone suggests in his chapter which closes the
book, the genuinely European cinema is not generally the cinema
which self-consciously seeks to be European but a variant of what
he calls, after Kenneth Frampton, 'critical regionalism'. This is a
cinema, rooted in the particularities of a specific culture, which
'replies' to the 'universalising' discourse of Hollywood's global
cinema in the accent of the local and the regional. Indeed, as
McLoone goes on to suggest, it may well be that this has always
been a predominant feature of the best European cinema.
Although it is common to think of European cinema in terms of
great individual directors or international movements in art (such
as modernism) it may be less appropriate to think in terms of one
unifying tradition of European cinema than of many local,
regional and national cinemas within Europe.

This is also of course an argument about democracy in the
broadest sense and of the importance of the cinema which is
available to us being able to speak for and to diverse social groups
and cultures. In this respect the argument for cinemas within
Europe is also a part of a broader argument for a greater plurality
and diversity of cultural output than are characteristically
provided by the international media economy. To some extent the
importance of this argument was recognised in the debate over
GATT. However, it is also true that in both Britain and Ireland this
debate often seemed remote and even irrelevant. In Britain, in
particular, the dispute was generally regarded as being almost
exclusively to do with the French. Thus, even the British trade
paper, *Screen International,* reported the outcome of the talks
under the headline, 'French celebrate GATT "victory"'.[5] The irony
of this, of course, is that the GATT talks were important not just
for France but Europe as a whole, including both Britain and
Ireland. To argue for the importance of European countries to
continue to make films, however, is not to be anti-Hollywood.
Certainly, there is no contributor to this book who doesn't watch
and enjoy Hollywood films. However, it is to argue against the idea
that Hollywood should be the *only* cinema. For while there may be
differences in emphasis and disagreements over priorities amongst
this book's contributors, what finally unites them is a belief in the
value of different kinds of cinema and not just one. The case for
European film-making (and indeed film-making around the globe)

is thus not only a case for cultural diversity but cinematic diversity as well. While this may be an argument that sometimes lacks resonance in a metropolitan centre such as London it is clearly of rather more urgency when placed, as this book is, in the context of cinematically peripheral areas such as Northern Ireland.

NOTES

1   For an overview of the main areas of dispute, see Mark Le Fanu and Neil McCartney, 'Fears grow over Gatt threat to EC audiovisual support policies', *Screen Finance*, 8 April 1992, pp.1–4.

2   See Julie Wolf, 'Gatt talks stumble on films and flying', *The Guardian*, 8 December 1993, p.15. Such levies are only employed by certain European countries and do not exist, for example, in the UK and Ireland.

3   *The Irish Times*, 15 December 1993, p.7.

4   According to figures cited by *The Guardian*, audio-visual exports (including not only film but also video and television) to Europe from the US totalled $3.7 billion in 1992 while the comparable figure for European exports to the US amounted to only $288 million. See 'Gatt: the movie', *The Guardian*, 8 December 1993, p.21. This represents an enormous leap from only four years before when it is estimated that the European deficit in audio-visual trade amounted to $1.8 billion. See *Screen Finance*, 18 October 1989, p.12.

5   *Screen International*, December 17–January 6, 1993/4, p. 1.

POLITICS, CULTURE AND CINEMA IN THE NEW EUROPE

Paul Hainsworth

Post-War Europe

Late twentieth century Western Europe has experienced an acceleration in the process of European integration. Despite persistent difficulties and disputes over a whole range of issues, the trend since the mid-1980s has been towards closer arrangements. At the forefront of this process have been key developments such as the 1987 Single European Act (SEA), ushering in the Single Market (SEM) or '1992', and the Maastricht Treaty. These landmarks are the latest stages of an unfolding and uneven dialectic. European integration rests upon various actors – such as nations, regions, parties and individuals – shifting their perspectives to fit a new and broader European setting. Basically, this integration is a post-war phenomenon, although historians have related the philosophic underpinnings – and, to some extent, the practice – back to pre-war and pre-twentieth century sources.

However, in the 1930s and early 1940s, any significant sense of Europe lost out to inter-state rivalry, nationalism, war and fascism. Against these, the pan-European Resistance Movement emerged as a laboratory and source of immediate post-war Europeanism. The actual moves towards integration derived from the conjuncture of several inter-related factors: the experience of World War Two and the Holocaust, the weight of European history (war, nationalism), the desire for socio-economic reconstruction, the emergence of two superpowers and the onset of an East-West bi-polar order. The 'European idea' resurfaced, therefore, as an attempt to redress the deficiencies of the past and to meet the imperatives of the present and future. As Beloff explains, 'the emergence of a strong movement for the reshaping of the European system on new lines was not simply a product of the international idealism foreshadowed in the previous

8

century but represented, rather, the recognition of an undoubted fact, the collapse of the old European balance beyond repair'.[1]

Amongst the first fruits of post-war reconstruction were the Brussels Treaty (1948) and the Council of Europe (1949) – the former of these two bodies was recast as the Western European Union (WEU) in the 1950s. Essentially, these organisations were inter-governmental rather than supranational, with the Council of Europe (COE) concentrating upon areas such as education and human rights and the Brussels Treaty/ WEU dealing with defence matters. More genuinely integrationist steps were the creation of the European Economic Coal and Steel Community (1951), the European Economic Community (EEC) and European Atomic Community (EURATOM) (1958) – all known collectively now as the European Union (EU). The latter incorporates different institutions to conduct the business of European integration: a decision-making Council of Ministers, representing national governments; a Brussels-based European Commission; a European Parliament and a Court of Justice.

From the outset, the integrative process has produced certain tensions which have served to focus debate, initially within elites but increasingly across a wider audience. These may be summed up as the conflict between sovereignty and supranationalism (or nationalism and Europeanism), between market and community and between an elitist and a peoples' Europe. Unsurprisingly, then, questions of identity have been central to European integration as nations, regions, social movements, political parties and individuals have endeavoured to construct, deconstruct and reconstruct their personalities vis-à-vis the emergent European reality. Here, one interesting example will suffice: the British Labour Party. Consider this odyssey: the party was opposed to membership of the European Coal and Steel Community – 'the Durham miners won't wear it' argued deputy leader Herbert Morrison; against European Community membership initially; an applicant in 1966; again against membership in 1973 – albeit 'unless the conditions were right'; divided in 1974–5 on the question of membership and offering a referendum to avoid the party having to make a formal commitment; reconciled to membership after 1975; contested the 1983 general election on a platform of withdrawal; came round to the idea of membership

subsequently; and, more recently, claims to be in the vanguard of
European construction.

Taking stock of Europe has become recently the preoccupation
of most social groups, professions and disciplines. The road to
1992 – and beyond – has been marked by a plethora of seminars,
workshops, conferences and colloquia, with contributors from the
cultural industries engaged prominently in the debate. In June
1991, the British Film Institute (BFI), for example, organised a
major conference on cinema in Europe. As Head of Research,
Colin MacCabe explained, 'questions of European media and
their relation to new forms of European and old forms of national
identity were placed at the top of the agenda'.[2] Indeed, those
responsible for the production of moving images recognise in
their art form an important terrain for negotiating questions of
identity. According to German film director Wim Wenders, the
'European art and language *par excellence* is cinema. There has
been no better expression of European identity in this century
than European cinema'.[3] Cinema can help to express the
complexity of contemporary European, national, sub-national and
international forms. In this respect, Duncan Petrie raises some of
the concerns at the heart of European political-cultural debate:

> the medium of cinema provides a unique means by which the
> cultural heterogeneity, diversity and richness characterising
> modern Europe can be rendered visible and cultural
> essentialism unmasked as a dangerous and reactionary fallacy.
> Cinema can help us to recognise the complexities of identity,
> including processes of transformation and change.[4]

Petrie visualises continental Europe as 'a seething pot of cultural,
national, regional, racial, political and social diversity' but
interprets the cultural crisis facing Europe as 'precisely the manner in which the idea of 'European identity' has been maintained
in opposition to the underlying diversity and heterogeneity'.[5] In
effect, therefore, Petrie's comments broadly support the thesis
that Europe is still perceived as too removed and homogenising,
too distant from popular concerns and particular constituencies.

To some extent, advocates of European integration are not
unduly discouraged by such perceptions since they believe the
problem lies in the presentation rather than the product and if
the latter can be packaged in a more attractive, user-friendly

format then Europe will emerge much more popularly as a positive symbol. In part to secure this end, the European ideal has been reconstructed critically under more imaginative labels such as 'a Europe of the regions', 'a citizens' Europe', 'a peoples' Europe' and 'a social space'. In addition, redress of the democratic deficit, economic and social cohesion, anti-racism and cultural provision have all become ingredients of the new Europe. Nor has the discussion been confined to an EC framework as other bodies and concepts have entered the debate, e.g., the European Conference on Security and Co-operation (or Helsinki process) and the European Convention on Human Rights, with their emphases on rights and freedoms, Gorbachev's 'common European home' and civil society watchdogs such as European Dialogue and Helsinki Watch.

In turn, political, bureaucratic and economic elites sponsoring European integration have been forced to address – not always successfully – the particular anxieties raised by accelerated integration and illustrated in recent referenda campaigns in Ireland, Denmark and France; by the lukewarm British attitudes to integration; by demands from the regions for increased funding from the European Structural Funds; and from labour organisations for a more active industrial policy. Within the 'new' Europe of the 1980s and 1990s European policy-makers have also turned to the question of culture, largely as a facet of the Single European Market but additionally as a means of bolstering the European idea. Indeed, the father of European integration, Jean Monnet, is known to have declared in his later years: 'If I had to begin again, I'd start with culture'.[6] In view of the contributions which follow this chapter, it will be useful here to assess the genesis, prevalence and nature of post-war European cultural policy-making – including its cinematic forms – before commenting upon the shape of the emergent Europe of the 1990s.

A cultural policy for Europe?
The initial attempts to channel a European cultural policy came through the Council of Europe and the Brussels Treaty/WEU. The Brussels Treaty – primarily a European mutual defence pact signed by the Benelux countries, France, and the United Kingdom – even described itself officially as a 'Treaty of Economic, Social and Cultural Collaboration and Collective

Self-Defence'. Article III of the Treaty declared that: 'The High Contracting Parties will make every effort in common to lead their peoples towards a better understanding of the principles which form the basis of their common civilisation and to promote cultural exchanges by conventions between themselves and by other means'.[7] From the start, though, some voices questioned the 'common heritage' approach as a rather sanitised and selective idealisation of Europe, and reservations persist. For instance, Roberts and Nelson maintain that the 'twentieth century has been European only in a negative sense. It is the story of self-destruction and division'.[8] According to Agnes Heller: 'Even if we add them together, European cultures (in the plural) do not add up to European culture. They were cultures in conflict, competition, or sometimes simply neglectful of one another'.[9] Barry Smart, too, sees Europe as 'a somewhat ambiguous geopolitical formation, one with a complex history, a problematic present, and an indeterminate future',[10] while John Keane queries: 'Is there such a thing as a uniquely European identity . . . ? The idea of Europe is a comparatively recent and highly contested invention'.[11] Nevertheless, definitional problems have not dissuaded proponents of European unity from mapping out some contours of a European personality. Etienne Tassin, for example, interprets the situation thus: 'Whatever the difficulties posed in defining a European *identity*, it is clear that the idea of Europe has denoted, and continues to denote, a common tradition of thought and culture rooted in that constant interchange over two millennia which has given this part of the world a certain unity of the mind'.[12] George Steiner also throws useful light on the identity question by accepting the European negative heritage as shared experiences but ones not to be repeated again: 'Europe shares a body of error, of remembered sorrow, of unspeakable self-destruction to the brink of suicide, in which there is perhaps also some hope. History might become the passport of shared identity, an actively lived and known history . . . We were so close to the possibility of there being no Europe at all'.[13]

Consequently, it is not surprising that European institutions have incorporated certain philosophical baggage in their founding charters. The Brussels Treaty preamble, therefore, stressed values such as fundamental human rights, the rule of law, political liberty and democratic principles as its basis. The Cultural

Committee of the WEU inherited this approach and persisted with activities such as the promotion and free circulation of art works, books and periodicals and the sponsorship of various cultural/artistic events. However, according to one informed participant, officials (drawn from Ministries of Foreign Affairs and Education) within the Cultural Committee 'had little idea of what they were trying to achieve'.[14] Even so, one institution of note was the Non-Commercial Cinema Sub-Committee, set up in 1949 to promote the exchange of documentary film, service film networks and sponsor central film libraries' acquisition of scientific and educational films. Possibilities for joint European productions were also discussed and, by the early 1950s, the sub-committee had facilitated its first European co-production, on a theme, landscape painting, intended to illustrate some of the best flowerings of Europe's common heritage. The film – leadingly entitled *The Open Window* – was exhibited at the 1952 Edinburgh Film Festival and other productions followed. For example, in 1958, the WEU-sponsored *December, Children's Month* won the Bronze Medal for short films at Venice whilst other WEU projects concentrated upon science, leisure, youth and teacher education.

Alongside the above initiatives, the Council of Europe (representing over twenty countries) promoted cultural-cum-artistic activity within the broad philosophical thrust of its mandate. The COE's founding statute declared that: 'The aim of the Council of Europe is to achieve a greater unity between its Members for the purpose of safeguarding and realising the ideals and principles which are their common heritage and facilitating their economic and social progress'.[15] Again, the realisation of these ambitions was not without controversy and the very first meeting of the COE's Consultative Assembly (with members drawn from national parliaments) wrestled with the conceptual term: 'in the interest of European unity'. Some voices argued that cultural cooperation was of value in itself, but political ideals and goals held sway, fuelling a debate which thereafter continued to mark European cultural provision.

The cultural concerns of the COE thus became languages, teaching, adult education, artistic and archaeological heritage *and* the promotion of a European unity and identity. As regards the latter, the COE sponsored a high-powered round table in 1953, which examined the spiritual and cultural aspects of Europe in historical and contemporary contexts. By 1962, the COE's Council for Cultural Co-operation (CCC) had emerged as the key cultural institution – also subsuming WEU cultural activities. The creation of this body marked a shift away from the original politicised orientation of COE cultural provision to a more narrowly focused role as 'an organ for educational co-operation'[16] and – in 1965 – the Committee of Ministers of the COE adopted a document, drafted by the CCC, entitled *The cultural policy of the Council of Europe.* The latter reflected the new orientation and foreshadowed the future direction of COE *and* EC cultural policy. While 'common heritage' and 'greater unity' figured in the document it strongly recognised the richness in diversity of European civilisation. In short, the now familiar 'unity in diversity' formula enjoyed a higher profile.

The CCC set up four permanent committees, including a Technical Committee for Film Activities which brought film specialists together, introduced a film prize for a European theme of artistic merit and pioneered a film week (in co-operation with Europe's film festivals) with the emphasis on short films. Various publications also followed including *Educational and Cultural Films: Experiments in European Co-production (1965)*, *The Use of 8mm Films in European Schools (1967)* and *Art of the Cinema in Ten European Countries (1967).*[17] In much of its cultural and educational work, the COE (like the WEU) worked with UNESCO – notably in the latter's major project for the mutual appreciation of Eastern and Western values – and other international bodies. In 1967, however, the COE streamlined operations and the film sub-committee was abolished. Even so, the CCC continued to relate to the film industry with emphases upon archival heritage, distribution, training, education, prizes, children's cinema and networking. By 1984, a COE spokesman could define the cinema as 'an important cultural factor and means of artistic expression and as an industry and commercial activity'.[18] This perspective lay behind the COE's creation of the Eurimages project in 1989.

Eurimages followed on from the promotion of cinema via the COE/EC designation of 1988 as European Cinema and Television Year. According to Eurimages' then Executive Secretary, Ryclef Rienstra, the project's role was essentially economic but also cultural. Hence, 'Europe must be encouraged to make its own distinctive contribution to film production. The price has to be paid if it is to defend its identity in the face of formidable American competition'.[19] Eurimages President, Gaetano Adinolfi, also highlighted 'the eminently cultural nature of the Fund, whose main objective is to support works which uphold the values that are part and parcel of the European identity'.[20] Adinolfi put into figures the price to be paid: Eurimages commenced in 1989 with a £5.5 million budget and over fourteen member states contributing. Neither the UK nor Ireland were founder members but both had joined by 1993 bringing participation up to twenty-three states. Eurimages has concentrated upon co-production, distribution, creative networks, documentaries and feature length films. The criteria to guarantee support from Eurimages encourages a European bonding in that independent producers must be drawn from at least three member countries. Interestingly, too, something of the ethos of the Council of Europe emerges in that projects 'with an obvious pornographic character or projects which clearly glamorise violence or contain an open appeal to the violation of human rights are excluded from any support whatsoever'.[21] The aim of funding is 'to attract the largest possible audience' and to consolidate the position of European films on national and international markets. Between 1988–92, Eurimages supported 144 European films, eighteen creative documentaries involving over 500 European producers and also supported seventy-three film distributors (involving thirty-one films). By 1993 the total of loans handed out by Eurimages had reached £55.5 million.

Eurimages literature takes pains to stress that it is not part of the EC's MEDIA scheme but nevertheless complements it. MEDIA is the by-product of the EC's relatively recent conscious preoccupation with the cultural dimension and this aspect is examined in the next section.

European Community: culture and film
Unlike the organisations discussed above, the EC commenced with little in the way of a specific cultural agenda. The founding Treaty of Rome (1957) looked forward to 'an ever closer union among the peoples' and liberal democracy served as a *sine qua non* of membership while the main thrust was economic and capitalist. With time, certain other features emerged more conspicuously, e.g., a European Regional Development Fund in 1974 to address imbalances, a directly elected European Parliament (EP) in 1979 to reduce the democratic deficit and, since the late 1980s, a

renewed emphasis upon the social dimension to offset the market orientation of the 1992 process.

As with the Consultative Assembly of the COE, the EC's European Parliament lobbied – notably in the early 1970s – for a greater cultural dimension and budget. Subsequently, EC cultural policy proceeded in three basic stages: (1) between 1977–82, the European Commission at least accepted a Community interest in the economic and social aspects of cultural provision; (2) between 1982-86, EC activity became more visible via 'a series of specific but disparate measures mostly symbolic in nature', e.g., architectural heritage[22]; and (3) since 1987, regular Council of Ministers/ Ministers of Cultural Affairs meetings have taken place with cultural activities, including the MEDIA programme, enjoying a higher profile.

Initially, good intentions were not matched by funding or much interest from the Council of Ministers, despite European summit meeting declarations – in the late 1960s and early 1970s – stressing the importance of promoting European awareness and mobilising culture as an expression of Europe's identity. In 1977, therefore, the Commission called for greater Council interest via a *communiqué* entitled *Community action in the cultural sector*.[23] However, the lack of response was underlined in 1982 by the title of a second Commission *communiqué*, *Stronger Community action in the cultural sector*.[24] As a result, one or two developments followed, e.g., the creation of an EC Youth Orchestra, but the Commission interpreted these as 'no more than a disjointed, poorly structured and clearly inadequate response to an obvious need'.[25] A third *communiqué*, *A fresh boost for culture in the European Community* (1987), yielded more fruits as the Council used it to establish four priority areas: the audio-visual sector, business sponsorship, books and training.[26] Subsequently, EC initiatives included the creation of a Cultural Affairs Committee, the designation of European cities of culture, conservation projects, support for creative networks and the MEDIA programme. A fourth and latest Commission *communiqué* endeavoured to take stock of and enhance cultural provision in the light of the Single European Market and the Maastricht Treaty, and the introduction is worth quoting at some length as a summary of the Commission's current perspectives:

The Community is on the threshold of a new era in which it will be able to grow beyond its purely economic dimension and enjoy unprecedented opportunity for cultural co-operation and support ... The challenge is two-fold: cultural action should contribute to the flowering of national and regional cultural identities and at the same time reinforce the feeling that, despite their cultural diversity, Europeans share a common cultural heritage and common values. The frontier-free area must provide a stimulating environment for intellectual life, cultural activities and artistic creativity for the ever-growing numbers of European citizens now demanding greater access to culture. In the face of growing intolerance the aim will also be to help them understand, appreciate and respect other cultures in the same way as their own.[27]

The document is revealing for several reasons. First, it endorses a unity-in-diversity and democratisation approach which has characterised much contemporary thinking on cultural provision. Second, culture is related firmly to the economic and wider environment of the current phase of European integration. Third, the Commission situates its call for mutual understanding in the context of growing intolerance, xenophobia and racism in Europe as illustrated by rising support for extreme right-wing political forces. This point was underlined by Commissioner Pinheiro responding to the Barzanti Report (see below) in the European Parliament.[28] Fourth, the approach urges a cultural dimension to be taken into account across EC policy-making. This represents a growing concern that the formulation of specific European policies should be examined for their *general* impact. For example, cultural policy is inter-related with areas such as social and regional policy, tourism, research, training and external relations. As Barzanti contends, 'culture must not be regarded as a curio to be relegated to a separate compartment but rather as a horizontal dimension that passes through the other policies and receives budget funds under whatever heading'.[29] This viewpoint receives some validation in Article 128 of the Maastricht Treaty. Fifth, EC activity is conditional upon the principle of subsidiarity which renders European cultural provision as a complement to, rather than a substitute for, national policy-making. This does not mean however that European film-makers need not look to Europe, for European sources help to make up the deficiencies in public and private funding. Even so, there were some fears within the EP that the subsidiarity principle might be used to stifle European initiatives. One intervention complained of 'constant statements of principle, scanty budgets, pilot experiments . . . as if to salve our consciences'.[30] Equally, there were anxieties that culture was being seen by EC decision-makers primarily as an economic product, thereby reinforcing the strictly market orientation of the EC. According to one critic, 'What shapes our ideas and our consciousness is not just the charm of supermarket shelves or the endless fight in the money-markets . . . It is the great culture of thought, art, philosophy, theatre, religious beliefs, ethics and style of our societies'.[31]

Last, and significantly, the Commission document makes no attempt to define culture beyond themes of diversity and general references to common cultural heritage. Indeed, this confirms existing policy since the 1982 *communiqué*, for instance, explained the approach: 'It does not expound a philosophy of culture, for that would imply coming out in favour of specific ideological and aesthetic options, which is something the Community has no right to do . . . There is no pretension to exert a direct influence on culture itself or to launch a European cultural policy'.[32] The intention rather is to treat film-makers and other artists as employees or cultural workers based on their socio-economic role. In the mid 1970s, too, the Council of Ministers had passed a resolution promising priority to measures likely 'to enable cultural workers to benefit as much as possible from social progress'.[33] Consequently, Fintan O'Toole is accurate enough in his assessment that 'the cultural dimensions of the Community's life have been notoriously bland: the European Ideal, our common heritage, a vague appeal to Europe itself as a moral and aesthetic category'.[34] The problems here are at least threefold. First, there is the nature of the EC as primarily an economic entity, albeit one tentatively taking on board other dimensions. Second, the EC has been reluctant to infringe upon the remit of nation-states or other international bodies in the sphere of cultural matters. Third, notwithstanding the mass of critical and constructive work done in the field of cultural studies in recent decades, culture *is* a difficult concept to define within a European framework. Raymond Williams, of course, recognised the problems: 'Culture is one of the two or three most complicated words in the English language. This is so partly because of its intricate historical development, in several European languages, but mainly because it has now come to be

used for important concepts in several distinct and incompatible
systems of thought'.[35]

Culture, then, is a late starter in EC policy-making and has been
engaged largely along the lines indicated. In this context, film
emerged as a suitable case for treatment. During the debate on
the Barzanti Report, for instance, Irish MEP Mary Banotti
expressed the need to 'look very seriously at the unsatisfactory
distribution of European films vis-à-vis the US competition'.[36] In
fact, the concern echoed European Commission worries in its
1982 *communiqué*:

> The cinema in Europe is facing special problems, from country
> to country ... Community-produced films have failed to
> establish themselves in distribution networks in the face of
> commercial competition from American-produced films:
> distribution of European-made film is not yet efficient enough
> on the world market, on the Community market and even on
> individual national markets.[37]

It was largely to address this problem – and the consequences of
accelerated European integration since the mid-1980s – that
Eurimages and MEDIA were launched. MEDIA is an important
component of the Community's audio-visual policy which
builds upon previous EC activities, e.g., business sponsorship,
distribution aids, film festival support and anti-piracy directives, in
order to meet the challenge of economic globalisation and the
Single European Market. Following on from a pilot phase, the
current MEDIA project rests on a five year programme (1991–95)
to stimulate European production with the emphases upon
competitivity, profitability and restructuring. With a budget of
around ECU 200 million and a soft loan policy, MEDIA has
promoted international successes, such as *Toto the Hero* (1991),
drawing upon specific cultural contexts. MEDIA's declared
strategy is to encourage market liberalisation whilst avoiding cultural uniformity:

> In the single market the European programme-makers will
> have to overcome a number of structural difficulties: producers
> are too small; production and distribution networks are too
> weak; language barriers have to be overcome. While the
> national basis of this industry provides a guarantee of cultural

diversity it also acts as a barrier to its development and limits the scope for cross-frontier distribution.[38]

The MEDIA programme therefore comprises several inter-related divisions designed to counter specific weaknesses in the production and distribution cycles (see Appendix). Amongst the main activities supported by the structures are production, distribution, exhibition, training, screen and scriptwriting, archives, animation, dubbing, sub-titling, creative networks and documentary work. British and Irish beneficiaries include Sally Potter's *Orlando* (1993), Joe Comerford's *High Boot Benny* (1993) and Pat O'Connor's forthcoming *Longshore Drift*.

All of these have been selected on the basis of commercial as well as cultural criteria. According to the detail of fund guidelines, MEDIA does not act as a 'crutch': 'The selection is severe to find agents which are likely to strengthen the industrial fabric of the market'.[39] The point is highlighted by Ben Gibson: 'MEDIA 95 programme is an industrial development programme, not a slush fund'.[40] Undoubtedly, though, the programme has provided much needed funds and, as McLoone suggests, 'offers considerable opportunities for broadcasters and independent producers in Ireland'.[41] Caughie, too, sees MEDIA as helping to open up the space in which peripheries can speak directly to each other.[42] Independent producer, James Mackay even places more confidence in European than in British funding.[43] Nevertheless, the dominant ethos of the EC – accentuated by the recent acceleration of the integrative process – has caused some practitioners to question the effects of European audio-visual policy. MacCabe, for example, considers MEDIA's European Film Distribution Office (EFDO) as 'entirely devoted to making sure it's possible to see more bad European films' throughout Europe,[44] whereas Irish film-maker Liam O'Neill raises a central question:

The tendency within the European Community's Media programme is almost exclusively towards the industrial aspects of filmmaking ... treaty priorities push EC policy towards economic rather than culturally driven goals. It is this bias rather than a true reflection of how film productions evolve that is enshrined in Media policy.[45]

This dichotomy between a culturally or industrially-biased cinema is at the heart of much contemporary film debate, and is a key theme of contributions below. As producer David Puttnam explains, 'film-makers are endlessly having to balance their natural desire to make lasting works of art against the need – even the desire – also to earn a reasonable living'.[46] Film director Joseph Losey extends the analysis: 'Film is a dog. The head is commerce and the tail is art. And only rarely does the tail wag the dog'.[47] Other voices are more confident about reconciling both sides of the equation. For instance, a Coopers and Lybrand Deloitte report in 1992 urged European film-makers to be more commercially aware of the international appeal of films whilst still reflecting the strengths of specific cultures – *Jean de Florette* (1986), *Cinema Paradiso* (1988) and *Cyrano de Bergerac* (1990) were put forward as examples of good practice.[48] Similarly, Colin Vaines argues that 'it is possible to develop scripts which have the thoughtfulness and intelligence of the best European cinema with the narrative, drive, energy and sheer accessibility of the best American movies'.[49] Certainly, MEDIA literature is very conscious of the American challenge to the European audio-visual industry. However, responding to the challenge draws a mixed response. John Friedman, for example, suggests that: 'We seem to have failed to understand that the Americans have found a better means of communicating the stuff of drama than we have'.[50] Consequently, he argues for a more accessible and less elitist formula. Yet, European attempts to cultivate an international market have their risks. The recent French film *Les Amants* (1992) was described by one critic as an extended Bounty advert whilst another confessed difficulty in separating the film from the advertisements![51] However, on the basis of three years of sifting through applications for funding, European Script Fund head Christian Routh was able to declare: 'I am beginning to feel confident that in two or three years time we will be witnessing the emergence of a new European industry that is rooted in its own culture, has little to do with America and is commercially viable'.[52]

Many observers will exhibit strong doubts about Routh's optimism – and justifiably so given the current increasing monopolisation of European cinemas by Hollywood products. Nevertheless, what unites many voices is a belief in the viability of a European cinema rooted in indigenous cultures, wary of incoherent Euro-puddings and offering alternatives to Hollywood images. Here is not the place to pursue these points in depth, but it will be instructive to recall briefly one or two interventions. For example, Mark Le Fanu maintains that 'the greatest European films have tended to emerge from within the context of strong, individualistic, national cultures. One hopes that increasing reliance on trans-European co-operation won't demolish this bedrock of national film production'.[53] Others such as Martin Bright[54] and Günther Plaum have made similar observations, the latter declaring no enthusiasm for 'Maastricht films'.[55] As Chantal Akerman argues : 'I don't think there is such a thing as European identity. The reasons why this question has arisen are, on the one hand, the increasing global domination of Hollywood, and on the other, the existence of the European Community and its ability to put money into European co-production'.[56] It is not that the baby should be thrown out with the bathwater: numerous voices have accepted Hollywood influences as very much part of film and popular culture, which benefits from comparison, inter-change and confrontation. Ultimately, though, we are back to the question of the tail and the dog with hopefully the tail enjoying more leverage. Conscious of Irish film-makers' dependence on external finance, Rockett insists that 'the space can exist from time to time in which the worst representational excesses of the Anglo-American film market can be contained'.[57] MacCabe sets out a more ambitious target: 'The question is not, I think, simply of making films; it's making films which actually then become part of the currency of intellectual and political debate within the culture'.[58] 'The culture' too is – as already suggested – a complex phenomenon which may incorporate different imaginings of Europe, nation, region and locality. After all, as McLoone explains, European identity is no less an artefact than national identity and the cultural-cum-cinematic challenge is neither surrender to 'the universal culture delivered by market forces' nor pursuit of 'a national essence through narrow and restrictive policy'.[59] These latter remarks point in the direction of analysis of the nature of the new Europe in which film (and other) debate takes place.

What kind of Europe?
The shape of the new Europe will have repercussions for film-makers and other citizens alike. Hence, one of the main issues raised in this volume – the character of national and/or

European cinema – will be influenced by how Europe, nation and region are perceived or imagined by producers and consumers. For instance, a strictly market approach may have its limitations. As Benedict Anderson states bluntly, 'in themselves, market-zones, 'natural'-geographic or politico-administrative, do not create attachments. Who will willingly die for Comecon or the EEC?' [60] Culturally, too, the market effect may reduce the scope of film provision to primarily Hollywood products or European imitations. Alternatively, market saturation and excessive commercialism may create an appetite for a different cultural diet, although this would depend on such factors as good distribution and exhibition outlets for European-made films. According to Lucia Rikaki, the audiences want to explore the richness of European culture.[61] Richness and diversity are then very much the theme of the Barzanti Report which pleaded the case for more cultural commitment:

> The European Union towards which progress is painstakingly being made will not emerge as the inevitable outcome of increasing economic integration or narrow monetarism ... This requires a more prominent role for the various types of cultural policy ... [and] ... Unless we respect national, re-gional and local differences there will be no policies capable of registering consensus, strengthening identities and encouraging an honest sharing of knowledge, stable exchanges and useful, fruitful collaboration ... The cultures of Europe are called upon to contend, together, with new exceptionally complex challenges. None will survive if it considers its future to depend on jealously guarding its past ... The idea of 'interculturality' has rightly been stressed, meaning not a generic multiculturalism resulting from a blend of cultures, but a relationship between realms, each of which has its own identity to protect and promote.[62]

The Barzanti Report has been quoted at some length since it serves as a pointer for future EU cultural policy: diversity is celebrated, essentialism unmasked, community is central and resources demanded. At the same time, it represents a critique of the current emphasis of the 'Europe-Open for Business' approach and a reflection of popular perceptions of the EC as centralised,

bureaucratic, remote and homogenising. Kearney, too, takes up
the cause of a culturally diverse Europe across the frontiers:

> European integration must not mean European uniformity . . .
> the task facing those concerned with our cultural future is to
> ensure that a Europe without frontiers does not mean a Europe
> without differences.[63]

'Unity in diversity' is not a new clarion call to European integration. Previously, it characterised the early post-war federalist movements which posed a decentralised, democratic, participatory,
peoples' Europe of the regions as an alternative to functionalist,
neo-functionalist, Marxist and other interpretations of
Europeanism. In the event, European federalism came up against
the rock of national particularism as personified by French
president Charles de Gaulle in the 1960s and Margaret Thatcher
in the 1980s. However, the concept of a Europe of, or for, the
regions now enjoys a second wind against the backcloth of
increasing integration, nationalist re-imagining and accelerated
globalisation. Current conceptualisations tend to release
regionalism from its reactionary-cum-conservative overtones and
reconstruct the concept as a postmodernist progression.

More recently, too, the debate about regions has incorporated
the concept of subsidiarity – 'an appalling word, describing
something very attractive and quite simple'.[64] However, this
concept has been open to so much interpretation that audiences
need to be conscious of who exactly is coining it. Basically, the
concept means decision-making at the appropriate level but
establishing this has proved controversial. Officially, this has been
interpreted as reasserting the national dimension. Nevertheless,
we can see emerging within the process of European integration
greater recognition of the regional dimension, notably via the
'economic and social cohesion' provision in the SEA and the
Maastricht Treaty's Committee of the Regions. Whilst the latter is
still the site of much speculation and too much should not be
expected of this consultative body, it will contribute towards
representing the complexity of European society. Interestingly,
the Commission's 1992 *communiqué* on culture formally invites the
Committee of the Regions into the debate. In an ideal Europe,
therefore, regional and local energies will be released in a
creative manner and this will have implications for cinematic

representations. Faced with change in Europe, Ien Ang thus predicts the opening up of 'space for the telling of smaller, more particular stories'.[65]

The corollary of these trends, then, is the downplaying of nationalism and the nation as exclusive, essentialist, immutable forms. This need not imply an unrealistic and contrived whisking away of the nation-state as a badge of belonging. Many strong advocates of regionalism, such as David Marquand, recognise the enduring power of the nation.[66] Yet, other forms of belonging have their attractions as the nation-state is perceived as an artefact. As Toby Miller contends: 'The nation is best understood as a constantly reformed remaking of tradition and coherence on an ever-altered terrain. The original account of the nation as "a body of people, with a common history and descent, a common language, common customs, and a long-standing attachment to a particular piece of ground" is no longer tenable'.[67] Anderson, especially, views nationalism or nation-ness as imaginings or 'cultural artefacts of a particular kind'.[68] Stuart Hall, in turn, sees national cultures as a distinctly modern form and discourse.[69] The notion of nation, Europe, culture and identity as properties permanently in a state of flux continues, therefore, to gain currency and was expressed eloquently by Edgar Morin: 'The organising principle of Europe can only be found in that historical principle which links its identity with perpetual coming and belonging'.[70] Elsewhere, Morin discusses individual and European identity, rooting the former in 'a cross-fertilisation and exchange between several concentric or polycentric identities'.[71]

Morin's ideas on cultural cross-fertilisation enable us to return to the question of 'what kind of Europe' from another perspective, for exclusion, alienation and marginalisation are part of the reality of contemporary integration. One problem is that representations of Europe and celebrations of European heritage and reference points may not satisfactorily account for the complexity of European identities. Ang strongly urges Europeans to come to terms with 'their waning cultural hegemony and to redefine themselves accordingly as particular rather than universal, as located rather than transcendental, specific rather than general'.[72] For Ang, 'the best bet for Europe to disentangle itself from its hegemonic past is to become post-European'.[73] MacCabe, too, suggests that 'it is the cultural reality of Europe which must be faced and faced urgently, if we are not to bungle the enormous possibilities offered by the growing movement towards political unification'.[74] For Edward Said, the challenge for Europe is 'not to purge it of all its outer affiliations and connections in order to turn it into some pure new thing' but rather to promote 'a kind of exchange of cultures that is not imperial' with more 'give and take than before'.[75] All these authors are perturbed by the prospect of Europe turning in on itself and marginalising groups in the process. 'Fortress Europe' in this context means lowering safeguards for minorities, refugees and asylum seekers. With the movement towards the Single European Market, civil liberties groups and migrant lobbies have pointed to increased state vigilance and discriminatory practices. As argued elsewhere, there is 'concern that sensitive issues such as immigration and asylum policy are being discussed in committees and councils outside the European Community's process of consultation and accountability, notably inside the Trevi Group, the Schengen Agreement and the EC's *Ad Hoc* Working Group on Immigration'.[76] The secrecy is compounded by tendencies to discuss immigrants in the same context as terrorists, criminals and drug-pushers, thereby automatically criminalising the former. There are fears that accelerated integration and the concept of European citizenship are in danger of creating second class citizens, i.e., immigrants. Against this background, film-makers have an important role to play in representing the anxieties and identities of marginalised groups and recent years have witnessed progress to this effect, e.g., Beur Cinema in France, black British cinema and immigrant representations in Germany.

While the market-orientated push towards a frontier-free Europe has repercussions for minorities, peripheries and socially disadvantaged sectors, even wider fears are expressed in the call for an enhanced social dimension and economic and social cohesion. For some critics, these latter aspects are mere palliatives to sweeten the bitter pill of increasing socio-economic disparities. From another perspective, championed by the British Conservative government, they are tantamount to increased bureaucracy, interventionism and supranationalism. The conflict between the two approaches has often pitted the British government against the European Commission with the latter demonised by the British pro-Conservative media. Liberal Democrat leader Paddy Ashdown even accused ex-prime minister Margaret Thatcher of placing Jacques Delors on the same pedestal as General Galtieri – the Falklands spirit could be applied to both – while Ken Coates explains how Delors was 'cast in the unlikely role of Marxist subversive'.[77]

Instead of viewing the EC as the site of interchange, compromise and dialogue, arguably too often a winners-and-losers discourse has marked Conservative policy. At Maastricht, for instance, John Major's much-publicised opt-outs, from the social chapter, economic and monetary union (EMU) and the word 'federalism', were interpreted widely as evidence of the UK's semi-detached European attitude, contrary to Major's declaration 'to put Britain at the heart of Europe'. Reporting back to the House of Commons on Maastricht, Conservative attitudes were illustrated vividly by Major's unashamedly triumphalist speech. Moreover, opinion polls demonstrated considerable public support for this Maastricht stance, despite some fears over the potential slide towards a two-tier Europe, with the UK in the slow lane of integration. However, Major's 'good for Britain, good for Europe' assessment was distinctly out of tune with other countries' perceptions. Moreover, anti-European sentiment inside the UK is nourished by unnecessarily confrontational posturing. The 1993 (October) Conservative Party conference was particularly marked by well-received xenophobic and Euro-bashing speeches from prominent cabinet ministers, leaving the normally supportive (to the Conservatives) Confederation of British Industry (CBI) professedly 'nervous about the way the debate in the Conservative Party has moved'.[78] Significantly, the CBI's annual conference followed the next month and was notable for speeches from Jacques Delors, Labour Party leader John Smith (who unsurprisingly exploited concern over government policy on Europe) and leading Conservative pro-EC 'heavyweights' (Kenneth Clarke, Michael Heseltine). Even invitee David Hunt, the Employment Secretary, explained that his party conference speech, attacking the social dimension of the EC, had been misinterpreted.[79] In effect, then, party rhetoric for rank and file consumption was followed swiftly by an exercise in damage-limitation before an audience at least largely sympathetic to the Conservative policy on social Europe. The social opt-out at Maastricht, of course, reflected the government's visualisation of the EC as more of a market than a community.

Certainly, workers in the cultural and other industries can draw little satisfaction from the refusal to guarantee them the same living and working conditions as their European counterparts. Kearney again views the prospects for Ireland: 'It will depend on whether we lend support to that current in European politics committed to narrow neo-conservatism ... on whether we take sides with the generous vision of Monnet, Spinelli and Delors or with the reactionary vision of neo-imperial nationalists like Mrs Thatcher'.[80] In fact, it could be claimed, not unreasonably, that implicitly Kearney overestimates the radicalism of the social dimension. This may be how certain quarters view it but it needs to be recalled that every nation-state except the UK opted into the social chapter at Maastricht. These included right-wing and centre-right forces as well as those left of centre. As David Martin explains: 'There is a remarkable consensus, even amongst politicians of the right, on the continent that we must build a social Europe'.[81] In truth, Conservative Party hostility to the social chapter is the product of an imagining of a Europe not easily recognised in the eyes of European counterparts. According to one analysis:

> The social chapter is a cautious and extremely generalised set of statements about the rules under which the European Community states can lay down policy on social affairs. It is not what it is cracked up to be. To pretend it is a trade unionists' charter, a dead hand of regulation in the affairs of the market, a socialist blueprint or even anything very different from the legislation already existing in most member states, even including Britain, is merely misleading.[82]

Nevertheless, despite the modesty of the social charter, it is still seen as an important cog in the European wheel. Without it, the European project is laid barer and reduced to the status of 'Europe Ltd'. As Delors contends, there can be 'no Europe without a social dimension ... 1992 is much more than a creation of an internal market abolishing barriers to the free movement of goods, services and investment'.[83] Yet, as the European Commissioner for Employment, Industrial Relations and Social Affairs, Padraig Flynn, pointed out recently 'the social dimension has not yet impacted on the minds of Europe's citizens to the same extent as the economic'.[84]

In conclusion, both the social and cultural dimensions might help to give meaning to an EU integrative process in need of sustenance to make it more accessible and acceptable to a wider audience. As José Vidal-Beneyto maintains, confining Europe's destiny to a large single market would be too narrow and an unacceptable regression.[85] Despite recurrent setbacks, European integration is still a hallmark of the future. But, to acquire genuinely popular and lasting support, it must recognise and respect the diversity and plurality of people's cultural identities whilst offering an accompanying social agenda. The social aspect helps to underwrite the notion of community by addressing the issue of living and working conditions whilst culture helps individuals and collectivities to make sense of and give expression to their lives. While Europe (or rather the EU) is but one player in this arena, the Maastricht Treaty at least provides a statutory basis upon which these dimensions may be promoted. Article 128, for instance, declares that: 'The Community shall contribute to the flowering of the cultures of the Member States, while respecting their national and regional diversity and at the same time bringing their common cultural heritage to the fore'.[86] Whether the challenge is taken up will depend not only upon Community aspirations but also on the political will of member states' governments and, of course, the human, creative resources within Europe.

APPENDIX: PROJECTS SUPPORTED BY MEDIA

Training

EAVE (European Audiovisual Enterpreneurs), Brussels.
MBS (Media Business School), Madrid.
These projects are designed to help professionals to improve their managerial skills and thus benefit from the potential of the large European market.

Improvement of production conditions

EUROPEAN SCRIPT FUND, London – support for writing and the development of screenplays.
SOURCES (Stimulating OUtstanding Resources for Creative European Screenwriting), Amsterdam – training workshops for European scriptwriters.

DOCUMENTARY, Copenhagen-Amsterdam – support for the development of creative documentaries as regards production, promoting and marketing.

CARTOON, Brussels – support for the creation and development of the European animated film industry, especially through networking of European studios.

MEDIA INVESTMENT CLUB, Bry-sur-Marne, France – support for audio-visual works using advanced technologies (computer graphics, digital and computer techniques in television, HDTV, interactivity).

SCALE (Small countries improve their audiovisual level in Europe), Lisbon – joint initiatives between countries with a limited geographical and linguistic area.

Distribution mechanisms

EFDO (European Film Distribution Office), Hamburg – aid for the distribution of European films in cinemas.

EVE (European video area), Dublin – support for the publication and distribution of cinematographic works on video cassettes.

GRECO (*Groupement européen pour la circulation des oeuvres*), Munich – promotion of the circulation of independent television fiction.

EURO AIM (European Organisation for an Audio-visual Independent market), Brussels – support structure offering services for the promotion of independent European productions on the international market.

BABEL (Broadcasting across the barriers of European language), Geneva – promotion of multilingualism in television programmes through financial support for dubbing and/or subtitling.

Exhibition

MEDIA SALLES, Milan and EUROPA CINEMAS, Paris – promotion of European films in cinemas.

EFA (European Film Academy), Berlin – centre for meetings and discussions open to professionals of the European cinema.

Contribution to establishment of a 'second market'

MAP-TV (memory/archives/programmes television) – development grants to promote audio-visual productions using audio-visual archive material.

LUMIERE, Lisbon – conservation and restoration of cinemato-graphic works stored in film libraries.

Stimulation of financial investment

EURO-MEDIA GARANTIES, Paris – risk-sharing with financial backers through guarantees on bank loans for European co-productions.

NOTES

1 M.Beloff, *Europe and the Europeans* (London: Chatto and Windus, 1957), p.63.
2 C. MacCabe, 'Foreword', in D. Petrie (ed.), *Screening Europe: Image and Identity in Contemporary European Cinema* (London: British Film Institute, 1992), p. vii.
3 W. Wenders, 'Europe seen from elsewhere', in R. Kearney (ed.), *Across the Frontiers: Ireland in the 1990s* (Dublin: Wolfhound Press, 1988), pp. 254–255.
4 D. Petrie, 'Introduction: Change and Cinematic Representation in Modern Europe', in Petrie, *Screening Europe*, p.3.
5 ibid., p.1.
6 See *Official Journal of the European Communities; Debates of the European Parliament*, 18–22 January 1993, no. 3 – 426/75.
7 Quotation from A. Haigh, *Cultural Diplomacy in Europe* (Strasbourg: Council of Europe, 1974), p.157.
8 D. Roberts and B. Nelson, 'Introduction' in B. Nelson, D. Roberts and W. Veit (eds.), *The Idea of Europe: Problems of National and Transnational Identity* (New York and Oxford: Berg, 1992), p.2.
9 A. Heller, 'Europe: An Epilogue' in Nelson et al, *The Idea of Europe*, p.23.
10 B. Smart, 'Europe Today and the Postmodern Paradox' in Nelson et al, *The Idea of Europe*, p.26.
11 J. Keane, 'Questions for Europe', in Nelson et al, *The Idea of Europe*, pp. 55–56.
12 E. Tassin, 'Europe: A Political Community' in C. Mouffe (ed.), *Dimensions of Radical Democracy: Pluralism, Citizenship, Community* (London: Verso, 1992), p. 171.
13 G. Steiner, 'Culture – The Price You Pay', in R. Kearney, *Visions of Europe* (Dublin: Wolfhound Press, 1992), p.53.
14 Haigh, *Cultural Diplomacy*, p. 159.
15 ibid., p. 193.
16 ibid., p. 214.
17 ibid., p. 226.
18 Claude Degand in *Forum* (Council of Europe Monthly), no. 2, 1984, p. XIV.
19 *Forum*, February 1991, p. 43.
20 ibid.
21 *Eurimages Guide* (Strasbourg: Council of Europe, 1993), p.8.
22 These are the words of the European Commission. See, *New Prospects for Community Cultural Action*, Communication from the Commission, COM (92) 149 final, Brussels, 29 April 1992, p.3.

23   *Community action in the cultural sector*, Commission Communication to the Council, 22 November 1977, Bulletin of the European Communities, Supplement, 6/77.

24   *Stronger Community action in the cultural sector*, Communication from the Commission to the Council and Parliament, 12 October 1982, Bulletin of the European Communities, Supplement, 6/82.

25   *New Prospects for Community Cultural Action*, pp. 2–3.

26   *A fresh boost for culture in the European Community*, COM (87) 603, 14 December 1987.

27   *New Prospects for Community Cultural Action*, p.1.

28   *Debates of the European Parliament*, 19 January 1993, no. 3–426/73–74.

29   ibid. cf. *Report of the Committee on Culture, Youth, Education and the Media* (Barzanti Report), 3 December 1992, PE 201. 819/fin.

30   *Debates of the European Parliament*, pp. 63–65.

31   ibid.

32   *Stronger Community action in the cultural sector*, pp. 5 and 14.

33   *Community action in the cultural sector*, p.26.

34   F. O'Toole, 'Culture and Media Policy', in P. Keatinge (ed.), *Ireland and EC Membership Evaluated* (London: Pinter, 1991), p. 270.

35   R. Williams, *Keywords: A vocabulary of culture and society* (London: Fontana, 1985), p. 87.

36   *Debates of the European Parliament*, p.73.

37   *Stronger Community action in the cultural sector*, p. 13.

38   European File, *European Community audio-visual policy* (Brussels:European Commission of the EC, 1992), 6/1992, p.6.

39   *MEDIA: Guide for the audio-visual industry* (Brussels: Commission of the European Communities, 1993), Edition 9, p. 7.

40   B. Gibson, 'Seven Deadly Myths', in D. Petrie (ed.), *New Questions of British Cinema* (London: British Film Institute, 1992), p. 31.

41   M. McLoone, 'Inventions and Re-imaginings: Some thoughts on Identity and Broadcasting in Ireland', in M. McLoone (ed.), *Culture, Identity and Broadcasting in Ireland: Local Issues, Global Perspectives* (Belfast: Institute of Irish Studies, 1991), p. 21.

42   J. Caughie, 'Becoming European: Art Cinema, Irony and Identity', in Petrie, *Screening Europe*, p.42.

43   J. Mackay, 'Low-budget British production: A Producer's Account', in Petrie, *New Questions of British Cinema*, p.63.

44   C. MacCabe, 'Final panel of Respondents', in Petrie, *Screening Europe*, p.73.

45   *Film Ireland*, November/December 1992, p. 8.

46   *Sunday Times*, 2 May 1993.

47   *The Guardian*, 20–21 February 1993.

48   *The European*, 22–24 May 1992.

49   *Info & News* (European Producers' Network/EAVE journal), no. 4, October 1992, p. 24.

50   *Info & News*, no. 2, April 1992, p. 5.

51   M. Bright, 'The death of the "auteur"', *New Statesmen and Society*, 19 June 1992, pp. 19–20.

52   *Info & News*, no. 4, October 1992, p. 7.

53   ibid., p. 19.

54   Bright, 'The death of the "auteur"', p.20.

55   Interview, *Film Ireland*, February/March 1993, p. 21.

56 C. Akerman, 'The Film-Makers Panel', in D. Petrie, *Screening Europe*, p.67.
57 K. Rockett, 'From Atlanta to Dublin', in *The Irish Abroad*, Foyle Film Festival programme, November 1992.
58 MacCabe, 'Discussion', in Petrie, *Screening Europe*, p.92.
59 McLoone, *Culture, Identity and Broadcasting*, p.25.
60 B. Anderson, *Imagined Communities* (London: Verso, 1992), p. 53.
61 *Info & News*, no. 5, February 1993, p. 15.
62 Barzanti Report, pp. 16–18.
63 R.Kearney, 'Introduction – Thinking Otherwise', in Kearney, *Across the Frontiers*, pp. 24–25.
64 N.Ascherson, 'Nations and Regions', in Kearney, *Visions of Europe*, p. 15.
65 I.Ang, 'Hegemony-in-Trouble: Nostalgia and the Ideology of the Impossible in European Cinema', in Petrie, *Screening Europe*, p. 28.
66 D.Marquand, 'Nations, Regions and Europe', in B.Crick (ed.), *National Identities:The Constitution of the United Kingdom* (Oxford: Blackwell, 1991).
67 T. Miller, 'National Policy and the Traded Image', in P. Drummond, R. Paterson and J. Willis (eds.), *National Identity and Europe* (London: British Film Institute, 1993), p. 103.
68 Anderson, *Imagined Communities*, p. 4.
69 S. Hall, 'The Question of Cultural Identity', in S. Hall et al, *Modernity and its Futures* (Cambridge: Polity Press, 1992), p. 292.
70 Quoted in Kearney, *Across the Frontiers*, p. 28.
71 E. Morin, 'Cultural identity in a global culture', *Forum*, no. 2, 1984, pp. 33–34.
72 Ang, 'Hegemony', p. 25.
73 ibid., p. 30.
74 C. MacCabe, 'A Post-National European Cinema', in Petrie, *Screening Europe*, p.10.
75 E. Said, 'Europe and its others', in Kearney, *Visions of Europe*, pp. 107–109.
76 P. Hainsworth, 'Introduction. The Cutting Edge: The Extreme Right in Post-War Western Europe and the USA', in P. Hainsworth (ed.), *The Extreme Right in Europe and the USA* (London: Pinter, 1992), p. 19.
77 K. Coates, 'Foreword', in J. Hughes, *The Social Charter and the Single European Market* (Nottingham: Spokesman, 1991), p. viii.
78 *The Guardian*, 12 November 1993.
79 *The Guardian*, 17 November 1993.
80 Kearney, *Across the Frontiers*, p. 18.
81 D. Martin, *Europe: an ever closer union* (Nottingham: Spokesman, 1991), p. 30.
82 *The Guardian*, 22 July 1993.
83 Quoted in Martin, *Europe*, p. 30.
84 P. Flynn, 'Foreword', in S. O'Cinnéide (ed.), *Social Europe: EC Social Policy and Ireland* (Dublin: Institute of European Affairs, 1993), p. vii.
85 J.Vidal-Beneyto, 'European Cultures = a European culture', *Forum*, no. 2, 1989, p.35.
86 Title IX. Culture. Article 128, *Treaty on European Union* (Luxembourg: Council/Commission of the European Communities, 1992), pp. 48–49.

IS THERE A EUROPEAN CINEMA?

Philip French

The question I have elected to address – 'Is there a European cinema?' – could be answered simply yes or no. However, I want to approach the question in a roundabout fashion and, although I will reach certain conclusions, it may well be that the evidence I present may lead readers, or some readers, to agree with the argument but to reach a different conclusion.

For nearly eighty years the British cinema has experienced a series of crises, or perhaps one should say that there has been one perpetual, extended crisis. Whenever that crisis has appeared to ease up slightly, a renaissance has been proclaimed by local observers. Italian culture has survived and triumphed with a single renaissance in a thousand years. The British movie industry has had at least four – in the mid-1930s, during World War II, in the early 1960s, and in the early 1980s. During all these years, and especially now, British cinema has been faced – as has the nation itself – with three choices: standing bravely alone in a post-Dunkirk-mode, throwing in our lot with the Continent, or depending upon the special relationship with Hollywood.

In mid-February 1993 the *Daily Telegraph* ran a poll to sample national morale and came up with the interesting revelation that, given the choice, forty-nine per cent of the population would like to emigrate. Clearly, this poll was not taken in Wardour Street or around Shepperton Studios, and does not reflect accurately the feelings of those in the movie business. Over fifty per cent of them have already emigrated and of those left behind ninety per cent would probably be happy to follow them. At the moment, due to a variety of factors – the strength of the dollar, the high quality of our domestic television, the unimaginative, virtually dim-witted policies of our distributors and exhibitors, the scandalous lack of support for film-making (indeed the positive disincentives) provided by the present government over the past fourteen years, and the apparent lack of enthusiasm on the part of native movie-goers for British films – we now have very little left in the way of a movie industry, despite the extraordinary pool of artistic and craft talent developed over the years (only Hollywood can match it), and not much either in the way of cinema.

Now the broad distinction I would make between a film industry and a cinema is this. A film industry is the totality of resources for the production of theatrical movies – the studios, laboratories and other services, the craft talents from electricians and carpenters to special effects people, editors, cinematographers, sound recordists and so on. Precisely what they work on and produce is not as important as the fact that they keep on working. For example, the most successful film company in Hungary is a studio set up in 1990 by the director Pal Sandor working on strictly commercial lines for the first time in that country and, apart from some local television productions, it is at present devoted exclusively to the production of foreign-financed films, mostly in English. A cinema, on the other hand, is the tradition of movie-making associated with a place or area, a body of work expressing, directly and obliquely, the spirit of its inhabitants, their character, aspirations, hopes and anxieties. A cinema re-creates and examines the past of the culture, reflects the present, argues about the future – it is an art form, a means of expression, a mirror, a source of shared experience. A cinema is cumulative, it has its own history and is part of the nation's history. It is possible to have a cinema without a movie industry. The Irish Republic has no film industry to speak of despite all the efforts to promote the Ardmore Studios, but there is clearly an Irish cinema that involves both the North and South and a vigorous Irish film culture. Moreover, in their book *Cinema and Ireland,* Kevin Rockett, Luke Gibbons and John Hill have restored a history and defined a tradition that were hitherto only vaguely perceived.[1] Even small, remote Iceland has recently been developing something in the way of a cinema, but it certainly has no industry, and the same is true of several of the Black African states that were formerly French colonies. It is possible to have a cinema in the past, but none in the present – as might be argued was the case in Australia before the sudden appearance of the New Wave around 1970. It is possible to have an industry without a cinema of any significance; this is certainly true of Germany between the end of World War II and the late 1960s. At least an industry can get by without making any notable addition to the notion of cinema as I've outlined it. The alternative Indian cinema as it grew up in the mid-1950s onwards has been largely divorced from the sub-continental industry at large. Satyajit Ray worked apart from the popular cinema of Bombay and this was not merely because he happened to live in Calcutta and speak Bengali.

There are legal definitions – for fiscal, contractual and statutory purposes – of what constitutes a British, American, Australian or French film, or any combination of these. Though until fairly recently a British film remained resolutely British by label (as a way of obtaining a subsequent award at the domestic box-office through the now defunct Eady Fund), Americans haven't worried too much provided the resulting picture appeared to be American. For the most part the movie-going public doesn't care and critics act according to the rule of the thumbs with which most of them write. For instance, the Indiana Jones movies were officially British productions, infusing American money into the country and employing local talent, but no one perceives of them as British. (The TV series about young Indiana Jones is being made in Czechoslovakia.) Likewise the film version of *Black Robe* (1991) about Jesuits in seventeenth century Canada (adapted from his own novel by Brian Moore – an Ulsterman with a Canadian passport living in California – and directed by an Australian) is a Canadian/Australian co-production. It was made entirely on location in Canada and assembled in Sydney, but no one would think of it as a contribution to Australian cinema, as opposed to a contribution to the eclectic oeuvre of the Australian director, Bruce Beresford. The same is true of *Lorenzo's Oil* (1992), shot in the United States with American money, but essentially a project of its Australian writer-director, George Miller and, like *Black Robe*, made with an Australian crew and with post-production at Miller's own studio in Sydney. John Huston's film of *The Dead* (1987), however, made in a Californian warehouse, strikes me as an entirely Irish film.

The need for national cinemas – or rather the recognition of such a need – was essentially a perception of dictators. Lenin called cinema 'the most important art' and before the Bolshevik Revolution had been won, film-makers were harnessing their talents in the interest of politics and the new national identity. So it continued to be for more than fifty years. Appreciating the power of cinema, those great movie fans Adolf Hitler and Josef

Goebbels immediately brought the cinema under party control when they came to power. In Italy, Benito Mussolini created the first film festival at Venice in 1932 to celebrate the greater glory of the new Italy, appointed his son Vittorio head of the film industry, and himself viewed every weekly newsreel before it was shown. The Fascists and the Nazis, however, were wiser than their Soviet counterparts and the ideological and propagandist works they sponsored – at least in the feature film area – were insinuated into a popular entertainment cinema in allegorical form, mostly through historical pictures. Where the British government intervened – other, that is, than to make the production of films more problematic through authorising the setting up of the British Board of Film Censors – was in the introduction of the quota system in the late 1920s which compelled British cinemas to show a proportion of British-made movies. This resulted in the production of, for the most part, mediocre low-budget pictures, the so-called quota quickies, which was like setting up poor preparatory schools and then neglecting to create secondary schools.

In America there was no thought of creating a national cinema. Indeed, most opinion leaders and upholders of public virtue saw the cinema as a threat to traditional American values – we must remember that the first two decades of the cinema coincided with the successful campaign to introduce Prohibition. One of the reasons explicitly advanced by the opponents of the burgeoning film industry to justify their hostility, and implicit in the antagonism of many others, is that the films were being produced by recent immigrants, most of them Jews from Central and Eastern Europe. This indeed was the truth. Seven of the eight major Hollywood studios were the creation of Jewish immigrants. Their role as innovators in a society that excluded them from more traditional occupations and professions, and their receptivity to talent from wherever it might come, shaped what we now call Hollywood. What they built was both American cinema and a world cinema. Their films were expressions of the American character and the American dream: positive, celebratory, though not uncritical, and made for a heterogeneous audience, the majority of whom did not have English as their first language. They created ideals of American life, provided myths of the nation's history. At the same time they were neither insular nor isolated. To a much greater extent than today, the settings were international, though with decreasing frequency did the film-makers leave the studio and California to make them. In this process they created a Hollywood view of Britain, Europe, the Orient, Africa and Latin America.

The two great talents of the silent Swedish cinema, Mauritz Stiller and Victor Sjöström were brought to Hollywood, and though neither prospered there for long, the effect was to bring to an end the first phase of the Swedish cinema. Between 1923, when Ernst Lubitsch made his first Hollywood picture, and the mid-1930s, virtually every major German film-maker, with the exception of G.W. Pabst, had emigrated to America – lured by Hollywood and in flight from Hitler. To what extent these emigrés became American directors depends upon subtle and not so subtle definitions. Their case, of course, is quite different from that temporary exile, Bertolt Brecht, who never ceased to be a German playwright, though he did try to be a Hollywood screenwriter. The director with the largest body of work in Germany and the United States, Fritz Lang, is the most important career we would have to consider. Alongside D.W. Griffith and Sergei Eisenstein, he is one of the seminal trio who created Western cinema. All three reached critical crossroads in the early 1930s, a major comparative study of their situations remains to be written. Offered (by Josef Goebbels) the post as head of Nazi cinema in 1933, the liberal half-Jewish Lang took as much money as he could reasonably withdraw without suspicion from his bank account, packed a few clothes into a small suitcase and took a train West. He made one movie in France, a skilfully crafted version of *Liliom* (1933), the Molnar play later musicalised as *Carousel* (1956), and then moved on to Hollywood. The subject-matter of most of his movies from his confident English-speaking debut, *Fury* (1936), onwards could scarcely be more American – gangster films, Westerns, thrillers – but the themes, the style and the signature remain consistent through out his life. He claimed to have had an access to optimism in America that eluded him in Weimar Germany – he thought his Hollywood films less concerned with death and destiny – but along with a generation of German emigrés (eg. Wilder, Preminger, Siodmak) he brought European preoccupations and manners to Hollywood.

The most perceptive American film critic of the 1940s, James Agee, poet, social observer, novelist, was the only reviewer to scrutinise closely – at the height of the war in 1943 – a clutch of pictures about European resistance movements. He makes crucial distinctions between the propagandistic projects of the American-born Irving Pichel's *The Moon Is Down* (1943) (a sentimental John Steinbeck script about the Norwegian Resistance shot on the sets built the previous year for John Ford's *How Green Was My Valley*, 1941), Jean Renoir's *This Land Is Mine* (1943) (Charles Laughton and Maureen O'Hara defying the Nazis in a manner Agee found 'dull, prolix and unamusing') and *Hangmen Also Die* (1943), the movie Lang and Bertold Brecht wrote about the assassination of Heydrich, the vicious *gauleiter* of Nazi-occupied Czechoslovakia, and its brutal aftermath. 'Of the three films, Lang and Bert Brecht's *Hangmen* is the most interesting', Agee writes:

> They have chosen to use brutality, American gangster idiom, and Middle High German cinematic style to get it across, and it is rich with clever melodrama, over-*maestoso* directional touches, and the sort of *Querschnitt* sophistication for detail which Lang always has. It is most interesting as a memory album. There's a heroine straight out of the Berlin of the middle twenties, and the Nazis are also archaic, nicely presented types: the swagger-ing homosexual, the cannonball-headed plainclothesman, the tittering, torturing androgyne who, one can imagine, is a revenge on some boyhood misery of Lang's in a Teutonic school. They are all conceivable, as Nazis; but they are all old-fashioned. The New Order has produced men of a new kind, and it would be more to the point to show some of them. [2]

Two other careers might well be cited, those of the two greatest movie-makers to be born in Britain, Charlie Chaplin and Alfred Hitchcock. It was both fortuitous and fortunate that Chaplin was in America in 1914 and got the chance to make movies. He would have had no such opportunity in Britain at that time. Hitchcock, however, was the most highly regarded director in Britain in the late 1930s when he accepted an offer from David Selznick – the best of several invitations that came his way – to work in Hollywood. Three of his first five films made there are set in Britain. That Hitchcock's American pictures are, as a whole, infinitely superior to his British ones scarcely needs arguing nowadays, though he was approaching the age of seventy and his career was almost at an end by the time that critics in the English speaking world came around to accepting this view. Chaplin, of course, didn't work in Britain until well after his prime, and the two films he made in his home country – *A King In New York* (1957) and *The Countess From Hong Kong* (1966) – are feeble things.

But neither Chaplin nor Hitchcock became Americans by an alteration in character and sensibility, though Hitchcock did, late in life, become an American citizen, thus denying himself the right to call himself Sir Alfred. I don't make this as a nationalistic or chauvinistic claim. My point is that their attitudes to class, character, behaviour and morality were shaped in London, as were their crafts – Chaplin's in the music hall and theatre, Hitchcock's in the theatre (as spectator) and the cinema (as practitioner). They came to maturity in America of course, and there is little question that neither would have realised his gifts with such power or reached such vast, universal audiences had they remained at home. Other British emigré film-makers have been more malleable – people like Robert Stevenson who went to Hollywood at the same time as Hitchcock and became a director at the Disney Studios. Those belonging to a later generation – like Ridley Scott and his brother Tony – were reared with an international popular culture and did not set out to bring anything distinctly British to Hollywood other than a loving eye for Americana.

You could say something similar about the Irish directors Pat O'Connor and Neil Jordan. O'Connor – with *The Ballroom Romance* (1982), *Cal* (1984) and *Fools of Fortune* (1990) – and Jordan – with *Angel* (1982), *The Miracle* (1990) and *The Crying Game* (1993) – have made major contributions to an Irish cinema. Their American movies, however, (O'Connor's *Stars and Bars,* 1988, and *The January Man,* 1989, Jordan's *We're No Angels,* 1989) have been without individual character – not even of the Irish-American kind. When Jordan, one of the most gifted directors of his generation, set out to court Hollywood with pleasing Irish stereotypes, the result, *High Spirits* (1988), though made in Ireland, is as bogus as the 1949 Bing Crosby-Barry Fitzgerald comedy *Top o' the Morning* (1949) where Hume Cronyn stole the Blarney Stone without setting foot outside the Paramount lot in Los Angeles.

While Hitchcock was ruling the roost in Britain during the 1930s, there were several Americans working in the small British film industry. I don't mean established Hollywood figures like Raoul Walsh and Josef Von Sternberg who made the occasional prestige picture in Britain. I mean directors of B pictures like Roy William Neil, Bernard Vorhaus (whom David Lean named as one of the most gifted people he worked with as editor) and William Beaudine. Their films featured English character actors from the West End stage and music hall comedians, country houses and home-counties villages, and seemed at the time, and now, quintessentially – indeed quaintly – English. Neil was originally slated to direct *The Lady Vanishes* (1938), a film which could not be more typically British; William Beaudine, now remembered if at all for his endless Bowery Boys comedies for Monogram Studio on Hollywood's Poverty Row in the 1940s, was responsible for the first distinctive Will Hay film, *Boys Will Be Boys* (1935), based on stories by J.B. Morton, best known as the long-time *Daily Express* humorous columnist 'Beachcomber'.

It might well be said that much of what was most British about domestic cinema in the 1930s was contributed by foreigners. The Hungarian Alexander Korda, after sojourns in Hollywood and France, came to England with his brothers, the director Zoltan, and the designer Vincent, to create Denham Studio and make movies that celebrated British history in a fashion and on a scale hitherto unknown. His first major success was *The Private Life of Henry VIII* (1933) and he followed it with a series of imperial adventure yarns that included *The Four Feathers* (1939) and *Drum* (1938). Apart from the contribution of his own family, he brought directors, designers and photographers from the States, and was an international producer par excellence. It was Korda who introduced the very English Michael Powell to the very Continental Emeric Pressburger and thus helped form one of the most extraordinary international partnerships in the history of cinema. You might well say, therefore, that Korda created a European cinema in the United Kingdom that continued intermittently until the 1950s. What is Carol Reed's *The Third Man* (1949), one of Korda's best late productions, if not a European movie? It could be argued that this tradition continued until the 1990s through David Lean, who worked for Korda on very British subjects in the early 1950s, and became a director of international epics after accepting Korda's advice. When Lean made his first American-financed movie, and his first proper excursion outside England, *Summer Madness* (1955), on location in Venice, Korda said to him: 'David don't go looking around the backwaters, go for the big effects, go for the Grand Canal'. That is just what Lean did for the rest of his life, and had he lived we would have seen his version of Conrad's *Nostromo*.

Lean, however, had grown up in a very *English* tradition as an editor, and continued in that tradition when he graduated to direction through his collaboration with Noël Coward. Perhaps the dominant, or at least the emblematic, figure in this area is Sir Michael Balcon, the head of Ealing Studios from 1938 until they were wound up in 1959, and creator of the Ealing ethos. Balcon had produced Flaherty's *Man of Aran* in 1933 and the following year transformed Hitchcock's then uncertain career by inviting him to direct *The Man Who Knew Too Much* (1934), the first thriller instantly recognisable as being in the Master's true style. Balcon worked briefly in Hollywood with MGM and then back home with MGM British, setting up the studio's trilogy of movies on very British themes that cast established Hollywood actors in leading roles – *The Citadel* (1938), based on the AJ Cronin bestseller; *Goodbye Mr Chips* (1939), from the James Hilton novella; and *A Yank at Oxford* (1938), based on an original screenplay. It was an unhappy experience for Balcon, with American directors being assigned to all three films and MGM executives constantly overruling him and often humiliating him. He left MGM after the first film (*A Yank at Oxford*) had been completed and shortly thereafter Balcon joined Ealing. Up to that time Ealing had been principally associated with the films of the Lancashire music hall artists Gracie Fields and George Formby, cheerful comedies of provincial life. Fields was in fact the biggest British box-office attraction of the 1930s and even made three films in Hollywood in an unsuccessful attempt to crack the American market. Formby enjoyed an almost equal success in Britain and in the Common-wealth and Empire (also oddly enough in Scandinavia where his style seemed to chime with local peasant humour), but he never got nearer the West End than the Dominion Tottenham Court Road, which in those days was where the moguls of Wardour Street thought the North began.

Following his bruising experience with MGM, Balcon set out quite consciously to create an autonomous British cinema and while at Ealing he never deliberately courted an American audience. His arrival just preceded World War II and in the early war years Ealing brought together the strongest tradition of the British cinema – the liberal humanist documentary – with the feature film by employing such stalwarts of the documentary movement as Harry Watt and Alberto Cavalcanti. J.B. Priestley, who through his BBC radio *Postscript* talks of the early war years spoke for the nation as powerfully as Winston Churchill, was also associated with the studio. He wrote one of the key movies of the first Balcon phase: *The Foreman Went to France* in 1941, a film highly critical from a working-class standpoint of the national leadership at the time of Dunkirk. He later had his play *They Came to a City*, a visionary work about the prospects for a post-war socialist Britain, filmed at Ealing in 1944. Although Balcon continued to make movies under the Ealing banner until 1959, the actual studio premises in West London passed into the hands of the BBC in 1955, the year of the last great Ealing comedy, *The Ladykillers* (1955). A plaque was put up at the entrance, the words written by Balcon himself. It read simply: 'Here during a quarter of a century many films were made projecting Britain and the British character'. I doubt if anything similar is to be found elsewhere in the world.

Already at that time the idea of what constituted British character was undergoing a profound change. Ealing's was a middle-class, liberal view of shared tastes and values: of respect for the monarchy, parliament, the armed forces and the law; a conviction that national institutions, while imperfect, were fundamentally sound; a belief that the imperial mission, for all its faults, had been a worthwhile undertaking, with lasting benefits to those who'd been its subjects; a liking for cricket, real ale, horse-racing, moderation, compromise and understatement. The so-called Angry Young Men of the 1950s were at this very time in revolt against national smugness, complacency, snobbery and hypocrisy (at its best Ealing evinced none of these vices, but it wasn't always at its best) and they were also against a national tendency to live in and dwell on the past, particularly the spirit engendered by the Second World War. These Angry Young Men were essentially serious, even solemn, yet not humourless, and they moved gradually from the political left to the right. They were followed by the satirists, who were fundamentally frivolous: after initially appearing to be radical, they eventually revealed themselves as apolitically opportunistic. The next wave – the public school ideological socialists – led by David Hare, Howard Brenton, Howard Barker, Trevor Griffiths and Stephen Poliakoff – were an altogether tougher, more determined group; they took over the subsidised British theatre and made inroads into TV and cinema, creating a political drama of a refined, rather detached and aloof kind that stood apart from popular culture and the population at large.

In the 1960s there arose a new conception of Britishness. The defiant working-class hero passed from the novel into the cinema in movies like *Saturday Night and Sunday Morning* (1960), *Billy Liar* (1963) and *This Sporting Life* (1963). This was followed by a change in style influenced by the French *nouvelle vague* and by Pop Art, two of the most notable, and now most dated, products being Dick Lester's two Beatles movies, *A Hard Day's Night* (1964) and *Help!* (1965). The link between these two phases is, or was, *Tom Jones* (1963) – the movie that is, not the Welsh pop star who took his name from Tony Richardson's film – which enjoyed an astonishing popular and critical success in the United States. Scripted by John Osborne, most celebrated of the Angry Young Men, *Tom Jones* went back beyond Victorian restraint and the Industrial Revolution to re-discover a freer, more exuberant national spirit that had supposedly been suppressed. That forgotten ebullience anticipated the so-called Swinging Britain of which the movie *Tom Jones* was the harbinger.

In 1962 the American statesman Dean Acheson famously remarked that 'Britain has lost an Empire but has not yet found a role'. Suddenly, the nation seemed to have discovered one as fashion leader to the international world of consumers : London had become, as I wrote at the time, the 'Alphaville of Admass'.[3] American movie-makers – still gagged by the Hays Office Code back home, depressed in the wake of the Kennedy assassination, worried over the escalation in Vietnam, and not yet having adjusted to the new youth audience – descended on Britain. Production boomed, the studios were working at full blast. Then after less than five years, Hollywood England started to crumble; first slowly, then suddenly. British cinema has yet to recover from those dangerous three or four years and the illusions they engendered.

A decade of anxiety passed before the next false dawn, or deceptively bright morning, that centred on the Goldcrest company. This affair is better documented than any comparable occasion in the British cinema and began with the surprise success in America of *Chariots of Fire* (1981). 'Watch out, the British are coming' said Colin Welland when he picked up his best screenplay Oscar in March 1982, a remark that proved almost as fatal and (according to Welland) as open to misinterpretation as Derek Bentley's 'Let him have it Chris'. With the success of Richard Attenborough's *Gandhi* (1982) the following year, it did indeed seem that they had arrived. The bubble burst four years later with the catastrophic and critical failure of both *Absolute Beginners* (1986) and *Revolution* (1985), two wildly expensive pictures that could only have shown a profit by a considerable success at the American box-office. But what were these movies? Based on Colin MacInnes's 1959 novel, *Absolute Beginners* was an odd-ball large-scale musical with a rock score recreating with little conviction the birth of British teenage culture and Britain's first race riots. *Revolution* was a bizarre interpretation of the American War of Independence, directed by an Old Etonian on locations in Norfolk, produced and written by Americans, with the leading roles played by an American (sporting an all-purpose celtic accent that US audiences found unintelligible), a Canadian and a German. As these films failed in America, an astonishing success was scored there by a low-budget film made for television that was rescued from the small screen due to the enthusiasm shown by the critics when it was premiered at the 1985 Edinburgh Film Festival. This was *My Beautiful Laundrette* (1985), one of a number of pictures from the mid-1980s that came to be grouped along with *The Ploughman's Lunch* (1983) in a new genre known as 'Thatcher's Britain' movies. This was a film dealing with a new political and cultural climate; and nothing better captures the puzzlement caused to some traditionalists, both by the film and the society it analysed, than the capsule comment on *My Beautiful Laundrette* by the late Leslie Halliwell in his *Film Guide* : 'Made for TV, but fashionable enough to get critical acclaim and cinema distribution, this soft-centred anecdote was a bit of a puzzle to those neither Asian nor homosexual'.[4]

The Goldcrest experience was an expensive way of learning that the American market offers no easy access to foreign movies. American cinema has indeed been changing over the near quarter-of-a-century since the big withdrawal from Britain around 1970. For one thing costs of producing mainstream features have escalated, jumping far ahead of inflation due to the costs of materials, the greed of stars and their agents, the popular demand for expensive special effects, and the budgets needed to advertise movies on TV. The cinematic life of films got increasingly brief as the 1980s wore on, so the need to make a large quick profit before a movie goes into the video shops became imperative. Everywhere, Hollywood productions have taken an increasing share of the market, not just in the UK where there is scarcely any sizeable appetite for foreign-language produce, but throughout Western Europe, including France (where until the last five years local films were most popular), and now Eastern Europe as well. At the same time there has been little continuity of leadership at the major studios and all but one are now partly or largely owned by Japanese conglomerates.

This has led to the recognition of a difference between Hollywood cinema and American cinema. There is a considerable, if fluctuating, degree of overlap, but essentially Hollywood is now the producer of expensive blockbuster productions designed for international audiences. It is significant that in December 1992 the Columbia Tri-Star film *A Few Good Men* (1992) opened simultaneously not only in nearly two thousand North American cinemas but also in more than thirty other countries around the world. Movies like *Terminator 2: Judgement Day* (1991), *Batman Returns* (1992) and *Dracula* (1992) are scarcely American at all: they are events within an international popular culture and in most countries outside the English-speaking world they are dubbed into local languages. They are what you watch between a session in a video arcade and having a Big Mac or a Burger King, wherever you happen to be.

The American cinema, once so much part of Hollywood, is now largely to be found in the modestly-budgeted independent productions of people functioning outside the industry proper or on its fringes, dealing with areas of society and experience neglected by the mainstream. These are the movies that are encouraged by the Sundance Institute started by Robert Redford and his associates. I'm thinking of such directors as Henry Jaglom, Gus Van Sant (*My Own Private Idaho,* 1991), Hal Hartley (*Simple Men,* 1991), Quentin Tarantino (*Reservoir Dogs,* 1992) to name but a few. Maybe some of the younger ones will become Hollywood directors. It isn't easy to say. Robert Altman, for example, now in his late sixties, moved into Hollywood and then drifted out, but is once again an insider, if a self-consciously subversive one. There was a belief in the mid-1970s that the so-called movie brats emerging from the film schools were going to take over and transform Hollywood. But what happened to Steven Spielberg, Brian De Palma, George Lucas, Francis Coppola and John Milius?

Hollywood took them over. The one that seems, in part at least, to have escaped possession is Martin Scorsese. As for Continental directors in Hollywood today, it's more important than ever to surrender to the system as the Dutchman, Paul Verhoeven and the Finn, Renny Harlin have demonstrated. A rare exception is Louis Malle, who made four remarkable, highly individual pictures in the United States, but fell down when he came to work within the studio system itself at Universal with the comedy *Crackers* (1983).

The split between indigenous American cinema and Hollywood has accompanied the social changes and recognition of cultural diversity that have produced new kinds of minority cinema. It is true that there was a small specialist audience in pre-war America for low-budget pictures in Yiddish or with wholly black casts, but such films more or less died out with the coming of World War II. Now there is a growing black cinema, a feminist cinema and, most recently, films directed at gay audiences, the self-styled New Queer Cinema. In these specialist areas within fragmenting societies, audiences don't make the same demands on the producers for special effects and elaborate production values that they make on the blockbuster productions.

As intimated above, all this is by way of preface to the question, 'Is there a European cinema'? More specifically what would it be defined against, and how would it be different from a British cinema? Is it something commercial? Is it an escape from the parochial? Is it a transcendence? Is it a search for some shared identity and culture – especially at a time when elsewhere nationalism is asserting itself in proud and virulent forms?

Most cinemas since the advent of sound have been defined initially by language, but in fact the Scandinavian countries, despite their four languages, have more in common than do the Spanish and Latin American cinemas or the Germans and the Swiss. In addition, as I've mentioned, most Continental countries dub foreign language pictures for all but a few metropolitan theatres, so for popular audiences foreign films don't have the exoticism of alien languages and sub-titles. For most of the post-war period the majority of pictures made on the continent have been financed by two or more countries and the concessions made by the producers to set up these co-productions have greatly varied. In some cases they're scarcely noticeable; they are often enhancing. A strong director together with the principal members of the cast will determine the movie's national character, irrespective of the setting. Directed by Italians with international casts on Spanish locations that purport to be nineteenth century Mexico or the American South West, the Spaghetti Westerns of the 1960s and 1970s now strike us as obdurately European and eventually came to glory in their Mediterranean provenance. But their origins were initially disguised by the English-sounding pseudonyms on the credit titles of the first crop of such pictures, which actually deceived, as they were intended to do, simpler members of their early audiences.

I think it right and necessary at this time that British film-makers should look to Europe – partly at least for the survival or salvation of British cinema. It would be absurd not to take advantage of the numerous organisations that exist within the European Union to facilitate the making of movies through development money for scripts and direct funding, as well as the organisations created for the distribution of movies, for providing subsidies to dub and sub-title films and to provide subventions for the wider availability of films on video cassette, both new films and those from the classic repertoire. In this sense European cinema does exist through these interlocking institutions, but it is not one that can be seen as a countervailing force to Hollywood and it would be dangerous to think that such a force could be created.

In the 1960s and 1970s in certain circles, all that was needed to bring anything or any concept into disrepute was to preface it with the word 'bourgeois', as in 'bourgeois truth', for instance, or 'bourgeois morality'. Certainly the prefix 'Euro' is being used to similar effect in the UK though not on the Continent. Those worried about pornography being beamed into the unsullied green and pleasant land of Britain speak of 'Europorn'. And the term 'Eurotrash' has come into use also to describe a certain kind of rootless production made in an odd form of English with an international cast and aimed hopefully, if vainly, at a world audience, meaning principally the United States. One thinks of recent movies like Claude Chabrol's *Dr M* (1989), starring Alan Bates, an attempt to update Fritz Lang's expressionist classic about the super-criminal Dr Mabuse in the reunited present-day Berlin, and the Fernando Trueba farrago *The Mad Monkey* (1990), starring Jeff Goldblum and Miranda Richardson. Most such films are still-born and go straight to video and off-peak television, or make a token appearance in cinemas on the way there. Such movies remind me of the short narrow street in Cannes that goes from the Croisette on the seafront under the railway line to a small back road. It runs only in one direction away from the main road, there are no doors opening onto it and therefore no addresses, and it is called the Rue Docteur Zamenhof after the Polish oculist Lazarus Zamenhof, inventor of Esperanto.

One should not, however, be put off by the failures in this area and retreat into a cultural isolationism. The fears created by 'European' pictures are shared by the French, who have a much stronger film industry than the British. While dubbing is the practice there, the organisers of the Césars, the French equivalent of the Oscars, have decided that no French film or co-production made in a foreign language (by which they really mean English) can qualify for a prize. The actors, directors and technicians can, provided they're French, but not the film itself. On the other hand, films thus disqualified aren't eligible for the prize for best foreign movie. There is little need for such a consideration in Britain as no one is likely to become substantially involved in a picture made in French, except of course for Channel Four, which has participated in the financing of films in a dozen languages and has invariably shown them on the small screen in the original versions. Channel Four has also backed several features in Welsh and one Scottish production in Gaelic.

What has traditionally kept foreign movies from wide distribution in Britain is the dislike of dubbing by critics and opinion leaders, and the rejection of sub-titles by the vast majority of the movie-going public, though oddly enough American and British moviegoers didn't object to the sub-titling of Soviet sailors in part of *The Hunt for Red October* (1990) or of Sioux Indians throughout *Dances With Wolves* (1990). To the best of my knowledge only two movies have ever received a full release in Britain with subtitles: Henry Georges Clouzot's *The Wages of Fear* in 1954 (when the Rank Organisation found itself short of product after its characteristically myopic refusal to equip Odeons with widescreens and CinemaScope lenses), and Jules Dassin's *Rififi* (1955) the following year (booked by the ABC circuit because the extended robbery sequence had no dialogue). Otherwise, foreign films were left to the ever declining number of independent cinemas that outside London have largely been replaced by community cinemas and regional film theatres. Language is much more important to British film-makers than to those of other countries. I am now inclined to think that if dubbing would bring foreign movies into circuit cinemas in Britain and thus to large popular audiences, and if this encouraged exhibitors to show popular Continental movies as well as art-house films – these are big ifs – then dubbing films should be encouraged. Certainly indigenous technical standards in this matter would need improving as they lag far behind those in France, Germany and Italy. Recently, a Portuguese producer/director took a full-page advertisement in *Variety* to write an open letter to Spielberg, Scorsese and Coppola suggesting that they honour their debt to European cinema and lend practical support to their professed devotion to foreign language films by giving up a couple of weeks each year to superintending the dubbing of a major movie of their choice for wide distribution in the United States.

There is therefore a European cinema to which we should subscribe, and perhaps it might appeal to a sense of intellectual adventure on the part of our moviemakers. In the original, genuine Renaissance of five hundred years ago, our artists felt themselves to be men-of-the-world without forfeiting a sense of national identity. Peter Brook has advanced beyond national boundaries in his theatrical work (and his best movie, *Moderato Cantabile,*1960, was made in French thirty years ago from a script by Marguerite Duras). Peter Greenaway has shown you can work with continental finance, Dutch designers, a French cinematographer and a mixed cast, and come up with a wholly individual product. Currently the most interesting film-maker in Sweden, with three feature films to his credit, is an Englishman, Colin Nutley, who chose the Continent rather than the United States (whereas his gifted Swedish contemporary Lasse Hallström moved to America on the strength of *My Life As A Dog*, 1985, but has only managed to complete one film there in four years). The Danish director, Lars von Trier, makes pan-European allegories utilising several languages, the most notable being his *Europa* (1991).

The Anglo-French production *Damage* (1992) gains enormously, I would say, from having a French director and a French leading actress. Ian Sellers' film *Prague* (1991) was made possible as a Franco-British co-production but the only concession demanded was a French actress (playing a Czech) and the movie establishes direct links of a plausible kind between Scotland and Central Europe. Bertrand Tavernier's film *Daddy Nostalgie* (1988), shown in Britain as *These Foolish Things*, is a truly European picture in the way that different languages – English and French – become part of the film's dramatic fabric. The same is true of George Sluizer's superb thriller *The Vanishing* (1990), where Dutch, French and English are used as part of the film's structure. It is sad, but not entirely surprising, that in order for *The Vanishing* to reach other than an art house audience in America and Britain, George Sluizer has re-made his own film in the United States with an American cast. This is in fact the surest possible way into the US market – make a successful picture on the Continent in a foreign language on a modest budget, then sell it to Hollywood to be re-made at greater expense in the States.

By way of conclusion, a picture which I suggest illustrates the theories alluded to above is Bertrand Tavernier's *Death Watch* (1979), a Franco-German co-production shot on location in Scotland. It is, I think, a genuinely European picture that has many of the qualities found in the classic Eurotrash production: wit, an international cast (from America, France, Germany, Sweden and Britain) all speaking English; a genre plot (in this case dystopian science-fiction) that touches on major themes; a stylised, undefined setting; a certain portentous air. (Of course much of that description would also fit *Casablanca*, 1942). But Tavernier, a knowledgeable, historically self-conscious film-maker, has actually chosen this dangerous international form and works through the unease it creates both to establish his futuristic setting, which is like, but not precisely, our own world, and to increase the tension between the characters. *Death Watch* is about the exploitative and intrusive qualities of the mass media, but it's also about voyeurism and how cinema makes voyeurs of us all, not just when we are watching, but in the manner that it conditions the way we view the world. At another level, and it is a very moral film, though not I think a moralising one, it treats of ways in which we can retain our personal respect and personal autonomy in modern society. But while these issues are intelligently, if sometimes laboriously worked out, the picture's real strength lies in the telling of an intriguing story, which doesn't flag until the final quarter of its length, which is some two hours and ten minutes.

This visually impressive movie can only be appreciated in widescreen in a cinema and it's lit by the gifted French cinematographer Pierre-William Glen, whose film school thesis, written under Bertrand Tavernier's supervision, was entitled *Psychoanalyse et Freudisme dans la série B américaine.* And Tavernier dedicates the movie to Jacques Tourneur, a distinguished director of American

B movies. He was the son of Maurice Tourneur, the first established European director to work in the United States – he went there in 1914 and became one of the major figures of American silent cinema. Jacques became an American citizen and apart from five years in France from 1928 to 1933, he worked in the USA and was a remarkable exponent of the low-key horror movies (especially in collaboration with the Russian-born producer Val Lewton), the Western and the film noir thriller. Such are the complexities and, indeed, ironies in the relations between European and American cinema.

NOTES

1   Kevin Rockett, Luke Gibbons and John Hill, *Cinema and Ireland* (London: Routledge,1988).
2   James Agee, *On Film* (London: Peter Owen, 1976), p. 35.
3   Philip French, 'The Alphaville of Admass', *Sight and Sound*, Summer 1966.
4   John Walker (ed.), *Halliwell's Film Guide* (9th Edition) (London: Harper Collins, 1993), p.828.

THE FUTURE OF EUROPEAN CINEMA :
The economics and culture of pan-European strategies

John Hill

Any discussion of European cinema must immediately contend with basic questions of definition: what is the conception of Europe which is being referred to and how is the cinema being defined? These are not simply pedantic quibbles. The idea of Europe is certainly not a straightforward one and even at the level of basic geography its boundaries are unclear and, with respect to the East, disputed.[1] And if the geography of Europe is blurred then its social, political and cultural contours are even more so, given the variety of national and ethnic traditions, political arrangements, languages, religions and cultural outlooks which are a feature of the European countries. Moreover, in the wake of the various social and political upheavals of the last few years, the idea of Europe as a social, political and cultural 'constituency' has begun to change and has undergone a number of attempts to re-think and 're-imagine' its parameters. If, as Stuart Hall argues, identities are never simply given, or complete, but are always in process then the identity of the 'new Europe' – as well as identities within Europe – are still in a process of 'becoming' and therefore belong, as Hall puts it, ' to the future as much as to the past'.[2] This is not, of course, to deny the importance of existing economic and political arrangements in the shaping of our ideas of Europe. Clearly the European Community (or European Union as of 1 November 1993) has cultivated a particularly strong and influential sense of Europe based upon its current twelve-nation membership and one, given the development of the MEDIA programme, which is of particular importance to the cinema.[3] But it is not the only European partnership of relevance to film. The Council of Europe, which predates the establishment of the EC, also holds a brief for the support of the audio-visual media and manages the European production support fund Eurimages which, by 1993, contained twenty-three members which included not only all the West European nations but also Poland and Turkey. The European Broadcasting Union, the European 'club' for public service broadcasters (many of whom have been involved in film production), is even more extensive with thirty-nine active members representing thirty-two countries stretching from Iceland to Morocco. Clearly then the boundaries of Europe, and hence European cinema, can, and have been, drawn in different ways.

But if Europe as a category is a contested one, is what is meant by cinema – and the idea of a European cinema – any more straightforward? Traditionally, in thinking about the cinema, three main areas of focus may be identified:

1) the economics and organisation of film production;
2) the nature and textual characteristics of films;
3) the distribution, exhibition and consumption of films.

However it is still relatively rare to find discussions of the cinema which take all of these elements into account. Government reports and policy documents, for example, characteristically focus on the economics of the film industry and tend to say little about actual films (or their aesthetics). Film histories and works of criticism, on the other hand, may elaborate upon the features of individual films or groups of films in great detail but still pay scant attention to the contexts in which they have been produced and consumed. What is then meant by cinema may not always be the same and may refer only to certain aspects of cinema activity. Moreover, the activities which have traditionally been seen as constituting cinema are no longer the same as they once were. This is particularly so given the increased blurring of the boundaries between film and television. Not only do more people now watch films on television and video than in cinemas but television finance has become a key factor in the business of making films. This is true of Hollywood but even more so of Europe. According to *European Filmfile*, 54 per cent of European films in production in early 1993 were backed by television finance and in certain individual countries the proportion was even higher (92 per cent in Portugal , 87 per cent in Sweden, and in the case of France, the largest film-producing country in Europe, 69 per cent).[4] Television funding is now central to European film production and any consideration of European cinema must take it into account.

However, even if all the various components of cinema activity are considered together there is still a potential difficulty in the way in which these may be identified as European. It might be helpful, in this respect, to distinguish the cinema in Europe from European cinema. For what is quite evident is that neither all of the films made, and certainly watched, in Europe could sensibly be regarded as European. Depending on the fluctuations of the international economy, Europe has often provided the location for the production of films which have been financed outside of Europe, have only involved small numbers of European personnel and which have lacked any recognisable European content. In the same way, the largest proportion of films actually viewed in Europe are not European at all but come from outside of Europe, mostly from the US. In this sense, therefore, it could be possible for there to be a successful European film industry which is nonetheless neither making nor showing European films. It is for this reason that Philip French, elsewhere in this volume, seeks to draw a distinction between the terms 'industry' and 'cinema'. For French, a cinema consists of more than simply film-making activities but also constitutes a 'tradition of movie-making associated with a place or area'. This is a valuable point to make and makes the attempt to link the characteristics of an industry to those of the films themselves. But how far is it possible to define a European cinema in this sense? Is there a recognisable film-making tradition which is linked to Europe the place (however defined) or are there simply individual authorial and national traditions within Europe? Does the label European identify any common formal and thematic features in films or simply provide a convenient peg on which to hang a variety of films with nothing in common other than their place of origin?[5] The idea of the 'European art film' has suggested there might indeed be a unifying European tradition but there are problems with this. First, it doesn't include what is probably the bulk of European film production and, second, it is the shared 'art' (non-classical narration, stylistic foregrounding, ambiguity and authorial self-expression) rather than any shared 'Europeanness' which seems to provide the category with its main unifying principle.[6] However, while it may be difficult to delineate a clear European tradition could European cinema, like Europe

itself, be in the process of 'becoming' and, as such, be an idea
worthy of support?

This last question has become increasingly important in recent
years as a result of the changes which the cinema in Europe has
undergone. The European film industry has entered a period of
decline and the appropriate response to this has become a matter
of some debate. This has involved consideration of both economic
and cultural matters: of both what economic measures are appropriate to restore the industry to health and what cultural outlook
European films should be encouraged to demonstrate. These two
matters are, of course, inter-connected for economic prescriptions will have consequences for the types and cultural characteristics of films which are made just as the enablement of films of a
particular cultural character will require particular economic strategies. What I would like to consider therefore are some of the
reasons for the current state of the cinema in Europe and some of
the solutions which have been proposed. In doing so I hope to
indicate the different conceptions of European cinema which
have been canvassed and what is at stake, both economically and
culturally, in them. I will then conclude with some remarks on the
particular case of Britain in relation to Europe.

At the root of the current crisis of European cinema are three
main factors: a decline in cinema audiences, a decline in
production and an increasing domination of the European
box-office by films from Hollywood. European audiences have
been in decline since the 1950s and during the 1980s this
downward trend continued. Admissions in every European
country fell, often quite dramatically (as in Italy where annual
admissions dropped from 241.9 million in 1980, the highest in
Western Europe, to 90.7 million in 1990). In the EC countries
overall admissions fell during the decade from 983.7 million to
564.1 million (and in Western Europe as a whole from 1,076.1
million to 621.9 million). (See Table One). The drop in Eastern
Europe was less dramatic during the 1980s but has now begun to
accelerate, with admissions dropping from 4,178 million in 1989
to 2,201 million in 1991, largely as a result of the growth in other
media outlets which followed the collapse of the East-West divide.[7]
Both the UK and Ireland witnessed an upsurge in admissions
towards the end of the 1980s but only to a limited degree. Thus, in
the case of the UK, the figure for 1990 (97.2 million) was still
below even the lowest figure for the 1970s and well below the

enormous totals of the post-war period (such as the 1946 peak of 1,635 million).

The consequence of these figures has been the same for most European countries: a drop in indigenous production. Thus, amongst the EC12 the number of films produced fell from 732 in 1965 (and 808 in 1970) to 617 in 1980 and 474 in 1990 with similar falls across Eastern Europe. (See Table Two).[8] Why this has occurred may be readily explained. Whereas it was once possible for European films in a number of countries to recoup their costs in their home markets this is now virtually impossible even for modestly-budgeted productions. According to a study by *Screen Digest*, only two European countries – West Germany and the Netherlands – generated a sufficiently large indigenous box-office share to cover the costs of indigenous film investment in 1988 and 1989 and this, they suggest, was due to the relatively low levels of investment involved (such that the Netherlands was responsible for only 0.5 per cent of total EC investment in 1988).[9] What has made this drop in theatrical admissions particularly damaging for European film industries is the difficulty they have faced in securing alternative markets for their films either in other countries or via other outlets such as video. European films have traditionally not travelled well and revenue from foreign markets has not been substantial. It is generally estimated that 80 per cent of EU-produced films are not distributed beyond the borders of their country of production and, of course, many of those which are, receive only a modest release.[10] Moreover, at a time when overseas distribution has become more important for European films, the evidence suggests that the opportunities for distribution in the US have become poorer. Thus, according to a survey in *Variety*, 245 films from France, Italy, Spain, the UK and West Germany received theatrical distribution in the US in 1967 compared with only 88 in 1987.[11] British and Irish film-makers, who have the advantage of sharing a language with the US, have traditionally looked to the US market with greater optimism than other European countries. However, success in the US has been erratic and has never provided a consistent or sufficiently substantial source of revenue. The UK share of the US box-office is characteristically around 1 per cent and, even in a good year such as 1992, no more than 3 per cent .[12]

The other weakness of the European industry has been its lack of access to the new outlets for film which have assumed so much importance since the early 1980s. It has become one of the paradoxes of recent film history that while audiences may be deserting cinemas they are actually watching more films than ever: they just happen to be watching them on television and video. The great triumph of Hollywood in recent years has been its ability to adjust to these new realities. Like Europe, Hollywood had to contend with the falling cinema audiences that ultimately led to the financial difficulties of the studios in the late 1960s and early 1970s. However, by the end of the 1980s, these problems had been successfully overcome and the strength of the major studios – Warner Bros, Disney/Buena Vista, Paramount, MCA/Universal, 20th Century-Fox, Columbia/TriStar and MGM/UA – was greater than ever. This is reflected in the growth in studio revenues from $2,495 million in 1980 to $11,392 million in 1990 which, even allowing for inflation, represents over a doubling of income. The key factor in this revival of the studios' fortunes was the ability to take advantage of the new television and video outlets for film. Thus, whereas returns from theatrical release (both domestic and foreign) accounted for 75.6 per cent of US studio revenues in 1980, the corresponding figure for 1990 was only 32 per cent. In contrast, revenues from Pay TV grew from 4.8 per cent to 9 per cent and, even more dramatically, revenues from video increased from 1 per cent to 45.3 per cent in the same period.[13] The pay TV and video markets have also grown in Europe (such that pay TV and video accounted for over 65 per cent of spending on film in Western Europe in 1992) but it is the US rather than the domestic film industries which have been reaping the benefits.[14] Foreign video and TV markets account for a substantial slice of US studio earnings (26 per cent in 1990) and, given its relatively high degree of video penetration, Europe provides a substantial proportion of this. As a result, the growth in the video market, which has been vital in restoring Hollywood to profitability, has not provided a similar source of revenue for the European film industry. The UK provides a particularly striking example of this. By the beginning of the 1990s, the spending on film on video was well over double the spending on film at the cinema box-office. However, the return to the British film industry from video has been negligible. In 1991, for example, US releases accounted for 93.7 per cent of video rentals while UK releases accounted for only 4.6 per cent.[15]

This domination of the European and UK market by Hollywood is the third major factor in the decline of European cinema. It has already been noted that while cinema admissions may have fallen the watching of films has actually increased in popularity. However, it is also the case that it is primarily Hollywood films which people have been watching. This is not only reflected in the figures for video but those for cinema admissions as well. Thus, between 1980 and 1990 the audience share for US films in the EC countries grew from 46 per cent to 69 per cent while in the UK and Ireland the US share was even greater (78 per cent and 76 per cent respectively).[16] These percentages are even larger when converted into box-office share. In 1990, the US share of EC box-office amounted to 77.4 per cent, in the UK 89 per cent and in Ireland 87 per cent. (See Table Three).[17] US dominance of Eastern Europe is also becoming an increasing reality. In 1991, for example, US films accounted for all but one of the top twenty films in Bulgaria, Hungary and Slovenia. In Poland they accounted for them all despite the fact that only the preceding year there had been just three US films in the top twenty.[18] What these figures also reflect is the intensification of control, on the part of the US majors, over distribution in Europe. The value of the overseas market has become increasingly important to Hollywood and the studios have combined resources to maximise its exploitation (most notably in the case of United International Pictures (UIP) which distributes films from Paramount, Universal and MGM/UA). In Europe it is only the Hollywood majors which have access to a pan-European distribution network and as a result they have been able to dominate the European market-place. One measure of their success is that, between 1985 and 1989, rentals from Europe to the US majors have increased from an estimated $301.6 to $702.5 million.[19] The bulk of films distributed are, of course, American and the evidence suggests that US distributors also favour US films at the expense of EC films.[20] The majors, moreover, have become increasingly involved in European exhibition (through the opening of multiplexes) and this has eased the passage of American films to European cinemas even more.[21] Of course, there is nothing new about US domination of European markets which dates back to the aftermath of the First World War. What is new, however, is its extent and the consequences this has then had for the viability of European film production.

As a result of these changes, all the national film industries in Europe have experienced broadly similar difficulties to which they have had to respond. Although shared, such difficulties have, according to Steve Neale, been traditionally conceived by the countries involved 'as a specifically national problem'.[22] However, this has been less obviously the case in recent years when the idea of greater international co-operation to resist Hollywood domination has gained considerable ground, particularly in a European context (although not exclusively so as the proposals for an English Language Cinema Plan have indicated). However, like the larger 'European debate', quite what form European co-operation should take, and what degree of integration it should involve, has not always been agreed upon and both 'minimalist' and 'maximalist' blueprints have been canvassed. Thus, one solution to the shared predicament of the European industries has been seen to lie in a pooling of resources and the creation of a pan-European industry which, it is believed, will stand more hope of success than any national industry on its own. Part of the impetus for this has come from the creation of a Single European Market which has been seen as creating a commercial space comparable of that of the US. Although the actual value of the film theatrical market is much lower than that of the US given the low rates of average attendances amongst West European audiences (about 1.78 visits per year) compared to their US counterparts (4.56 visits), the population of the EC12 at 325 million is substantially larger than the US population of 247 million. Moreover if the West and East European markets are added together this provides a level of admissions and box-office which overtakes that of the US. As has already been indicated, the problem with these figures from a European point of view is that US films enjoy the predominant share of both markets. Nonetheless, it is the *potential* a unified European market is believed to hold which has fuelled many of the hopes for a revived European film industry.

Such hopes have both economic and cultural implications. Historically, national cinemas have been faced with the choice of a) attempting to compete directly with Hollywood, b) relying primarily on the domestic market for commercial viability or c) aiming at more specialist outlets both nationally and internationally. However, given the decline of national theatrical markets, it is argued that it is now Europe as a whole which can provide a European film with a 'home' market of much greater size than any individual national market and, indeed, of comparable size to that of the US. Thus, it is argued that economic success does not necessarily depend on breaking into the US market and that the European market on its own is sufficiently large to sustain European film-making. However, in order to take advantage of this new European market, it is also argued that European films will need to change their character (and become less 'specialist'). In comparison to Hollywood films, European productions are predominantly 'low' and 'medium' budget. Thus, despite the drops in European production levels, the EC12 still maintained a comparable level of production to the US at the end of the 1980s : in 1990, 474 films were made in the EC (and 559 in Western Europe) compared to 438 in the US. However, the level of average investment was substantially different: $2.84 million in Europe versus $7.99 million in the US.[23] The discrepancy would, of course, be even greater if the European figures did not include US-financed productions and the US figures were restricted to the output of the Hollywood majors. Thus, the estimated average cost of a studio film in 1990 has been put at a total of $38.8 million ($26.8 million negative cost plus $12 million advertising cost).[24] The conclusion that is often drawn from such figures is that the budgets of European films are too low to allow them to succeed outside of their national markets. Thus, in 1992 Eurimages announced its intention to support projects with higher budgets on the grounds 'that there is a direct relationship between the size of the budget and the number of the territories in which the film can be sold'; and this was reflected in its decision to lend to a Danish/German/Portuguese co-production, *The House of Spirits* (1993), shooting in English on a budget, at £11.3million, well above the European average.[25]

This, John Hopewell suggests, may be seen as part of what he calls ' a growing consensus' that 'a future European film industry' should 'generate more, higher budget pictures' intended to recoup 'their costs from international territories rather than just from a release in their own country of origin'.[26] Certainly there are now a number of reports which have advocated this viewpoint. Although not its main recommendation, the British Screen Advisory Council report, *The European Initiative: The Business of Film and Television in the 1990s* did nonetheless canvas the view that 'instead of producing a large number of low-budget films it (Europe) may be better advised to produce a smaller number of more expensive films so that producers can afford to spend substantial sums on promotion and marketing ... throughout Europe and worldwide'.[27] The former Chief Executive of British Screen, Simon Relph, has also argued, along with Jane Headland, that if 'the European opportunity' is to be seized then European film-makers 'must create industrial structures which rival the power of Hollywood as well as make films with their own European stars'.[28] Two other reports put the case even more strongly. *European Film : industry or art?*, a report by Coopers and Lybrand, laments what it calls 'the self perpetuating circle of low-budget films' (low-budget = small audience = low revenue) and calls for an 'Empire Strikes Back' policy which will challenge US domination of Europe on the basis of greater European co-ordination, the encouragement of European 'majors' (and a European studio) and a more commercial orientation.[29] In *Europa Europa : Developing the European Film Industry*, a Media Business School publication, Martin Dale claims that 'Europe has not aimed at or understood the mass international market' and should be making European films which follow 'the simple principles of American movies'.[30] In another report for the Media Business School, *The Competitive Position of the European and US Film Industries*, London Economics are rather more cautious about recommending one particular approach over another but do nonetheless give serious consideration to both a 'European' strategy of pan-European production and even an 'international' strategy of integrating with the US film industry.[31]

It would be unfair to these reports to suggest that they are unaware of the economic obstacles to the implementation of their ideas (or that they do not allow for different types of film-making activity within Europe). Nonetheless , it does seem the case, that they over-state both the feasibility and desirability of their proposals.The economic might of the Hollywood majors is linked to so many factors – the scale of their production, the concentration of resources and deal-making activity in Los Angeles, the size and relative homogeneity – compared to Europe – of the US home market, the successful penetration of 'ancillary' markets and the ownership and control of an international network of distribution and exhibition interests – that it is virtually impossible to conceive how any European strategy, even if it could be successfully co-ordinated, could overturn such competitive advantage. This is the more so given that the re-orientation of the European film industry which is envisaged would not simply be an economic matter, involving changes in methods of financing, production and distribution, but also a cultural one, involving a particular approach to the films to be made. For where all the reports above agree is that European film-making should also change in character and become more 'commercial' and more obviously aimed at the 'mass market'. However, this is a more complex matter than the reports suggest.

As has already been noted, the prescriptions for change do not envisage, at least in the first instance, an attempt to break into the US market. It is the size and potential value of Europe as a 'home' market that is seen to provide the basis for a more commercial pan-European industry. As such, it is not proposed that European films should directly imitate Hollywood films. 'Whenever European films attempt to ape American models', writes Dale, 'they are hollow and fail both artistically and commercially'. He therefore argues for the development of 'new European models'.[32] Similarly, Coopers and Lybrand do not advocate a switch to 'purely US style product' but recommend films which will have 'an international appeal' within Europe.[33] The difficulty, however, is in identifying what these films might be, particularly as it is the limited appeal of European films outside of their own borders which is regarded as the central problem which a pan-European industry must overcome. Dale, moreover, is critical of attempts at big-budget European film-making which might at first glance appear to conform to his prescriptions. Thus, he is critical of Goldcrest for making *Absolute Beginners* (1986), *The Mission* (1986), and *Revolution* (1985) on inflated budgets. These films, he argues, were made on the assumption that they were 'generalist fiction' when they were in fact only 'targeted fiction'.[34] Of course, what is meant by 'generalist ' fiction, in this context, is really fiction which will appeal to the 15-25 year old age group who constitute the largest proportion of the cinema audience, rather than any genuinely 'mass' audience. Audiences for European films have traditionally been older than the Hollywood average and one of the problems high-budget European productions have faced in the past is their failure to appeal to sufficiently large numbers of the young. David Puttnam, for example, has cited his own production *Meeting Venus* (1990) as an illustration of this.[35] Dale is no doubt right to be sceptical of the financial sense of expensive middlebrow productions with limited 'crossover' appeal . However, his own prescriptions for a 'revolutionary new kind of European cinema' based on 'universal' appeal and a shared European heritage is itself quite problematic.

Dale's argument is that the success of Hollywood in Europe is due to its successful use of universal themes which have a global appeal. There is certainly something to be said for the argument that part of Hollywood's success overseas has resulted from the ethnic mix (including immigrant Europeans) of its domestic audience and hence the adapting of its films to a more variegated audience than any other national industry (although, given the persistent demands for more diverse representations within Hollywood films, this is an argument which can be over-stated). However, this is not quite the same as saying that Hollywood films then have a 'universal' appeal, for 'universality' cannot be separated from the universal presence that Hollywood films have enjoyed since the 1920s as a result of Hollywood's economic power internationally.[36] What appears to be universal in this respect may actually be the consequence of familiarity. Moreover, there is considerable evidence to suggest that, while the appeal of Hollywood films may be widespread, the pleasures which they provide and the meanings which they offer are more varied and socio-culturally specific than the notion of 'universal appeal' would allow. Indeed, one of the pleasures for European youth provided by Hollywood films has often been its very difference from (and sometimes challenge to) the European cultural context in which it has been viewed.[37] Without a tradition of familiarity (and generic evolution) comparable to Hollywood and a cultural context which is sympathetic to it, it is therefore unlikely that European cinema can simply expect to tap into some source of 'universal' appeal (and given the strain which the 'universalising' discourses of European thought have been under in recent times there may be something insensitive about expecting it to).[38]

Of course, the second part of Dale's argument is that Europe should be able to provide such a context and that, despite the various linguistic, ethnic and national divisions that characterise Europe, there is still sufficient of a common European identity to sustain a popular pan-European cinema. Indeed, in his conclusion, he goes so far as to claim that it is diversity which has been the weakness of European films and that they must now find 'common themes and reference points'.[39] What these might be, however, is left vague and Dale is at a loss to identify much more than a shared goal of 'freedom' and some common obsessions with class, politics and national identity (which may well provide shared points of reference but are also experienced in quite particular and potentially divisive ways). The issue here is one that has been debated more generally in relation to European media policy. There has, for example, been considerable scepticism, particularly in relation to official EC rhetoric, about the existence of a supranational European culture or identity which it might be the job of the European audio-visual media either to defend or represent. There has also been a questioning of how adequate the dominant definitions of European identity actually are given their characteristic associations with whiteness, colonialism, Christianity and high culture.[40] Accordingly, it is difficult to see what reservoir of common cultural symbols a popular pan-European cinema might draw upon, particularly given the importance of 'high art' (both classical and modern) to the prevailing sense of European cultural identity. It is one of Dale's arguments that Europe should seek to recover what he regards as a lost 'tradition of popular fiction'.[41] However, popular European cinema, as Dyer and Vincendeau point out, has characteristically been the most national of European cinemas and the most confined to its own borders, due in part, they suggest, to the great importance of language to popular genres such as comedy.[42] The decline, as Dale sees it, of European popular fiction is therefore largely the result of the decline in the national cinema audiences necessary to sustain it and, of course, its subsequent migration to television where national programming still remains of such great importance.[43]

According to Ien Ang, 'a genuinely popular European cinema seems to be an impossibility'.[44] Her point here is actually to do with the irony and self-consciousness which she sees as characterising even those European films which strive to be 'popular' but it may have a more general validity. For the 'impossibility' which she identifies results from the national and cultural specificity of European popular traditions and the absence of any pan-European popular sensibility which could sustain a popular European cinema. The popular cinema which Europe shares emanates from Hollywood and Europe possesses neither the economic means nor the cultural resources to compete with it successfully. Indeed, it could be argued that the economics which now underpin Hollywood have made clear-cut distinctions between American and European cinema more difficult. For

Hollywood now operates on a more global scale than ever, providing films which are often less 'American' than transnational in character. Europe is now almost as much Hollywood's 'home' market as the US itself and many Hollywood films perform significantly better in Europe than in the States. Europe therefore features more strongly in Hollywood calculations and, as Ilott suggests, films are increasingly tailored 'to suit foreign audiences as much as Americans'.[45] The central product of the Hollywood studios is therefore the relatively rootless global 'event' movie which is increasingly divorced from the specificities of US experience. Indeed, as French suggests elsewhere in this volume, it is the gap now created by the event movie which has encouraged the emergence of a low-budget US cinema devoted to exploring contemporary US realities. It is therefore all the more ironic that so much thinking within Europe should be committed to ideas of competing with Hollywood or, as in Dale, developing its own 'global' fictions. For it is precisely the many spaces which Hollywood leaves empty that European films would most usefully be involved in filling.

Indeed, what is often absent from calls for a European 'fight back' strategy is any clear rationale of why this should be so desirable. What often animates such demands is simply indignation that Hollywood should command such a large proportion of European box-office or, even less helpfully, a refusal to accept that, in the case of film, Europe is not a world leader. However, if it is only a matter of economic clout and standing in the international market-place then there is the possibility, as indicated by London Economics, that Europeans simply opt for closer ties with Hollywood. Hollywood may have been increasing its global power but it has also been becoming increasingly international not just in its output, as noted above, but also in its ownership and operation. This has been most obvious in the acquisition of major studios by the Japanese but Europeans have also played a role. European banks have been responsible for financing Hollywood (and in the case of the state-owned French bank Crédit Lyonnais controls MGM); European companies (such as the French Canal Plus and Ciby 2000, the Dutch Polygram, and the Italian Penta) have all done deals with Hollywood; while European stars and directors have happily worked there. If Europe wants to become a major player in film then economic logic suggests continuing along this route makes the most sense and there are already European audio-visual companies with sufficient financial muscle to operate on a global scale.[46] Obviously, such an option will not answer the other concerns which the current state of the European film industries has given rise to, namely the consequences for the cultural output of Europe of Hollywood's domination of European screens. However, as should be evident from the preceding discussion, it is not at all clear that the defence and encouragement of European cultures will be well served by the project of a pan-European cinema either.

What unites the film industries in Europe is not any common European identity that a pan-European cinema can draw upon but rather a shared situation and set of problems which certain forms of European co-operation may help alleviate. As Ian Christie has suggested, the unity to which the European film industries should aspire is basically a strategic one based upon 'common need' rather than a common culture.[47] Two key developments – the EC's MEDIA programme and the growth of European co-production – give some indication of how this strategy can operate (despite some appearances to the contrary). Given its stated objective of 'creating a European audiovisual area', the MEDIA programme has often been characterised as a policy which seeks to develop a pan-European industry capable of competing with Hollywood.[48] Indeed, Dale goes so far as to claim that 'the EC initiative has declared itself to be Europe's first Major'.[49] However, this is a somewhat misleading characterisation of MEDIA's activities which operate on a relatively modest budget of around ECU 50 million per year and do not (except in a small way via SCALE) involve direct support for production. The main thrust of the MEDIA programme, in this respect, has been less concerned with forging a supranational industry than with 'promoting', as its documentation puts it, 'national industries at Community level' through various forms of assistance (in areas such as training, development and distribution).[50] Evidence of this use of European resources to enhance the viability of national industries is provided by the support which is given to the distribution (through EFDO and EVE) and exhibition (through SALLES and EUROPA CINEMAS) of national films across European borders. The objective, in this respect, is not to create pan-European films but rather to lay the basis for a pan-European distribution and exhibition network.

The growth of European co-productions also illustrates the potential for national industries to pool resources. Estimates, for

example, suggest that while only 24 (out of 781) films made in
Western Europe in 1975 were international co-productions this
figure had risen to 203 (out of 552) by 1991.[51] In the same year 23
out of 49 UK films produced were international co-productions,
including a large proportion with European partners.[52] This
increase is evidently a result of the difficulties which national
industries have faced. Co-production has not only increased the
amount of production finance which is available to the European
film-maker but has also reduced some of the film-maker's
financial risks by enhancing the opportunies for distribution and
financial returns in the co-producing countries. However,
co-production also has its pitfalls.The financial involvement of
more than one country has exerted pressures on the types of
projects which have been put together and the resulting films have
often paid the price in terms of a loss of cultural specificity and the
incorporation of a number of spurious pan-European elements.
This is a tendency which the desire for a big-budget pan-European
cinema could continue to fuel but it is not an inevitable
consequence of co-production which can also be used to produce
films genuinely grounded in European and national realities.
However, this is most likely to occur, as Ed Buscombe suggests,
when 'finance is derived from various countries but production is
essentially controlled by one'.[53]

What has been suggested so far is that the enthusiasm, in some
quarters, for a big-budget pan-European cinema is
misplaced. For while cinemas in Europe share problems in
common the solution to them does not appear to be the creation
of a common cinema. Rather it is through the mobilisation of
transnational resources in support of national and regional
cinemas rooted in specific cultures that the cause of a genuinely
European cinema would be most successfully advanced.
Nonetheless, within Europe, film policy still remains significantly
national in character and many of the arguments which
characterise debate about European cinema are also played out at
a national level. This is particularly so of Britain where the sense of
identity with Europe has characteristically been more troubled
than in other European countries and where the relationship with
the US has often been perceived as stronger.

Of all European countries it is Britain which has hankered the
most after success in America and has sought to compete in the US
home market. Attempts to crack the States date back to the 1930s,

and the efforts of Alexander Korda, and have been repeated on various occasions since.[54] During the 1970s and 1980s, Rank, Thorn-EMI and Goldcrest all sought to make films for the US market and all did so with disastrous results. Ironically, at the time of Goldcrest's collapse (precipitated by the three high budget projects already mentioned : *Absolute Beginners, Revolution,* and *The Mission*) a number of much more modestly-budgeted films were finding success in the US (such as *Room With A View,* 1986, *Mona Lisa,* 1986, and *My Beautiful Laundrette,*1985). However, this too proved a short-lived trend when the US independent distributors which had sustained it found themselves in financial difficulties as a result of increasing competition from the majors. However, despite this unpropitious record the British industry is still reluctant to admit defeat. Indeed, the 1993 Oscar nominations for *Howards End* (1991), *The Crying Game* (1992), and *Enchanted April* (1991) (all films which did well in the US but much more modestly in Britain) have helped to revive the belief that British films might yet be world-beaters.[55] This belief has in turn conditioned some of the attitudes which are then taken towards Europe.

Such a belief, for example, animates the view that it is Europe which holds out the possibility of a re-constructed British film industry aimed at the US and that it is Britain which is the country most advantageously placed to be the hub of a 'pan-European' cinema. This is perhaps best summed up in the idea of Britain as 'the Hollywood of Europe' which has been attributed to Lew Wasserman, the former head of Universal and surprise participant in the Downing Street seminar on the British film industry, chaired by the then Prime Minister Margaret Thatcher in June 1990. Indeed, it has been suggested that Mrs. Thatcher's own belated bout of enthusiasm for the film industry, following years of neglect by her government, was precisely such a vision of 'Britain as the future centre of European film-making'.[56] It is an idea which has also been expounded by the Director of the BFI, Wilf Stevenson, in his preface to to the *UK Film Initiatives* series. In this he argues that, for European film-makers, 'it makes sense to try to break into the US market' and that the UK, standing at the crossroads between the United States and Europe, is therefore the natural home for a European cinema which wishes to export its products 'to the biggest market in the western world'. He therefore concludes, in a remark entirely free of the spirit of European co-operation, that it is the UK which 'stands the best chance of winning the battle within Europe to dominate the film market'.[57]

The problems with such formulations are, of course, manifold. If British films have traditionally failed to succeed in the US there is no particular reason to suggest that European films made in the UK in English are likely to do any better. Nor is there a great deal of evidence that European film-makers will want to. Indeed, the film policies of countries such as France have been designed precisely to defend the making of films in their own languages. Moreover, as has been seen, even proponents of a big-budget pan-European cinema do not envisage the US as its primary market but rather an enlarged European one and as such would not necessarily see the UK as its most desirable home. Dale's strongest candidates for a centre of European film-making, for example, are Paris, Berlin, Barcelona and Milan.[58] As Ben Gibson suggests, Britain's claims to be at the centre of European film-making are not based on a commitment to Europe at all but rather on 'an idea of being more American than other Europeans' and hence of being less, rather than more, European than other countries.[59]

There has also been an element of spurious 'Europeanism' in some of the other appeals which have been made to Europe. What has been evident is that, along with Ireland, the UK has been until recently one of the European film industries least well-served by national government. During the 1980s, the Conservative government, led by Mrs. Thatcher, removed the quota for British films, abolished the Eady levy (designed to return funds to production), 'privatised' the National Film Finance Corporation (subsequently British Screen) and put an end to the tax incentives which had fuelled much of the investment in film in the early 1980s. It was not surprising therefore that, by the end of the decade, investment in film had declined, the number of films made had dropped and US domination of the domestic box-office had increased.[60] This weakness in the production sector of the industry engendered a certain envy of the systems of support available in other European countries (especially in France and Germany) and Europe was increasingly used as a yardstick by which to measure the health of British production. As a *Screen Digest* survey of state aid in the EC countries observed, the British government's 'flight from interventionism' appeared to go against Community plans for 'harmonisation' of trade practices and it became a recurring complaint that British film-makers suffered from the lack of 'a level playing field' in Europe.[61] Indeed, the force of this argument was finally conceded when the UK government belatedly agreed to finance a European Co-production Fund, to be administered by British Screen, and then to pay the subscription to Eurimages, the last Western European country to do so. A specific incentive in the case of Eurimages was, of course, the fact that Ireland had already joined and therefore looked set to reap the benefits of being the only member of Eurimages to have English as an official language.[62]

While these are important developments there is also a sense in which they emerged under the pressure of necessity rather than from real commitment to Europe. Terry Ilott, for example, has suggested that much of the British enthusiasm for Europe in the early 1990s stemmed from the experience of failure in the US and was largely oblivious to the cultural aspects of a re-orientation towards Europe.[63] There is also little doubt that the appeal of European co-production for the Conservative government had more to do with the prospects of attracting European film-makers to Britain (possibly with a view to making films in English) than with helping British film-makers become more successful with European audiences. This is not, of course, how the policy of the European Co-production Fund, which has even shown itself willing to back films other than in English, has actually been implemented but there is still a strong sense, nonetheless, that the British film industry remains reluctantly European and still hankers after transatlantic success.[64]

This is not to say, however, that Europe necessarily provides an answer to the British film industry's problems or that films self-consciously aimed at European audiences are especially desirable. Certainly, as Ben Gibson has argued, British producers do need to explore further the market for a more 'European' kind of British film but the evidence suggests that this is likely to be a kind of film which is also specifically British.[65] As even the British trade paper, *Screen International*, has acknowledged the most successful European initiatives appreciate that 'international funding can be spent on very local projects' and that 'the best local films derive their appeal from their cultural specificity', citing as examples, in the case of Britain, both *Riff-Raff* (1990) – winner of the European Film Award for Best Film in 1991 – and *Edward II* (1991).[66] As these two examples suggest, the contemporary British film, in order to have European appeal, need not be particularly expensive (*Riff-Raff* cost £0.75 million, *Edward II* £1.1 million) and can maintain both a level of artistic adventurousness and socio-cultural complexity.

Moreover, it is precisely such socio-cultural complexity which is the hallmark of a genuinely 'national cinema'. As I have suggested elsewhere, the traditional conception of a British 'national cinema' as in some way expressive of a unified 'British culture' or 'British way of life' is no longer adequate (if, indeed, it ever was).[67] Rather the 'national' cinema, which is properly 'national', must be capable of registering the lived complexities of 'national' life, be sensitive to the realities of difference (of nation, region, ethnicity, class, gender and sexual orientation) and alert to the fluidity, as well as assumed fixity, of social and cultural identities. It must also recognise the increasingly hybrid and relational character of cultural identities both within the 'nation' and between nations. In a sense this then brings us back to the question of European cinema. I have been critical of the idea of a synthetic pan-European cinema and have argued instead for the importance of cinemas (national, regional, local) in Europe. This is not to suggest, however, that the 'European' and the 'national' are then locked in opposition. Rather, it is to indicate that what common European identity there is, or might be, only co-exists alongside and intermeshed with the nationally and culturally specific. Ironically, therefore, the experience of 'being' or 'becoming European' might be precisely one of the areas which a national, or nationally specific, cinema could and should address.

Table One

CINEMA ADMISSIONS: 1960-1990 (millions)

	1960	1970	1980	1985	1986	1987	1988	1989	1990
Belgium	79.56	30.39	20.65	17.87	17.73	16.08	15.22	16.07	17.10
Denmark	43.92	23.86	15.90	11.30	11.40	11.50	9.96	10.30	9.62
France	354.67	184.40	174.80	175.00	167.80	136.70	124.70	120.90	121.90
German Fed Rep	604.80	167.40	143.80	104.20	105.20	108.10	108.90	101.60	102.50
Greece	61.20	128.60	42.99	23.00	22.00	19.50	17.00	17.50	13.00
Ireland	41.00	20.00	9.50	4.50	5.00	5.20	6.00	7.00	7.40
Italy	744.80	525.00	241.90	123.10	124.87	108.84	93.13	94.79	90.70
Luxembourg	4.50	1.30	0.80	0.70	0.70	0.60	0.50	0.50	0.54
Netherlands	55.44	24.14	25.58	15.30	14.80	15.50	14.80	15.60	14.60
Portugal	26.59	28.00	30.80	19.00	18.40	16.90	13.70	11.55	11.00
Spain	370.00	330.86	176.00	101.10	87.30	85.70	69.60	78.10	78.50
UK	500.80	193.00	101.00	72.00	75.70	78.40	84.00	94.60	97.20
EC	*2,887.28*	*1,656.95*	*983.72*	*667.07*	*650.90*	*603.02*	*557.51*	*568.51*	*564.06*
Austria	106.50	32.90	17.50	13.30	12.60	11.20	10.00	10.30	10.20
Finland	24.60	11.70	9.90	6.70	6.30	6.50	6.70	7.20	6.20
Iceland	..	..	2.60	1.40	1.30	1.30	1.10	1.20	1.24
Norway	35.00	18.58	17.50	12.90	11.10	12.37	11.65	12.60	11.40
Sweden	55.00	28.20	24.00	17.90	16.60	17.50	17.50	17.00	14.54
Switzerland	40.00	32.00	20.90	16.40	16.30	16.00	14.90	15.20	14.30
other W Europe	261.10	123.38	92.40	68.60	64.20	64.87	61.85	63.50	57.88
all Western Europe	*3,148.38*	*1,780.33*	*1,076.12*	*735.67*	*715.10*	*667.89*	*619.36*	*632.01*	*621.94*

Source: *Screen Digest*

Table Two

FILMS PRODUCED 1965-1990

	1965	1970	1975	1980	1985	1988	1989	1990
Belgium	1	4	9	6	7	15	10	20
Denmark	18	20	18	13	9	16	18	13
France	151	138	162	189	151	137	136	146
Germany	72	113	73	49	64	57	68	48
Greece	96	88	38	27	27	19	8	..
Ireland	1	5	2	5	2	5	3	3
Italy	188	235	198	163	89	124	117	119
Luxembourg	..	0	0	0	1	1	3	1
Netherlands	1	4	16	7	13	10	13	21
Portugal	..	8	16	9	9	16	7	9
Spain	135	107	110	118	77	63	48	47
UK	69	86	69	31	47	40	27	47
EC	732	808	711	617	496	503	458	474
Austria	21	7	6	4	12	9	11	14
Finland	9	13	5	10	15	14	10	13
Iceland	..	..	0	3	5	2	2	2
Norway	11	11	15	10	12	9	10	12
Sweden	21	22	14	20	17	21	26	25
Switzerland	10	5	30	13	34	20	16	19
rest W Europe	72	58	70	60	95	75	75	85
total W Europe	804	866	781	677	591	578	533	559

Source: *Screen Digest*

Table Three

US FILMS' SHARE OF NATIONAL MARKET 1980-1990

	1980	1981	1982	1983	1984	1985	1986	1987	1988	1989	1990
	%	%	%	%	%	%	%	%	%	%	%
Belgium	47.0	48.0	43.0	52.0	54.0	68.0	72.0	62.0	64.0	68.9	73.5
Denmark	44.5	45.0	70.0	53.0	70.0	61.2	65.5	65.8	71.0	63.6	77.0
France	35.2	30.8	30.0	35.0	36.8	39.1	43.3	43.8	45.9	55.3	56.9
Germany	54.9	52.9	55.4	60.4	65.8	59.0	62.6	58.3	64.4	65.7	84.8
Greece	58.0	56.0	51.0	56.0	63.0	76.0	79.0	81.0	85.0	86.0	87.0
Ireland	88.0	87.0	86.0	84.0	83.0	83.0	85.0	86.0	82.0	85.0	87.0
Italy	33.7	32.6	32.0	41.6	47.6	48.6	51.3	48.1	56.0	63.1	69.4
Luxembourg	60.0	60.0	62.0	62.0	64.0	65.0	65.0	65.0	65.0	64.0	65.0
Netherlands	46.2	46.0	51.4	51.9	60.5	74.3	78.6	63.9	75.0	78.0	82.0
Portugal	46.0	56.0	44.0	47.0	48.0	51.0	64.0	67.0	72.0	81.0	85.0
Spain	35.0	50.0	50.0	50.8	53.8	58.4	64.1	58.4	64.2	71.4	72.5
UK	88.0	85.0	82.0	78.0	81.0	84.0	86.0	89.0	77.0	84.0	89.0
EC	..	..	..	..	..	64.0	..	..	68.5	72.2	77.4

Source: *Screen Digest*

NOTES

1   See, for example, Philip Schlesinger, 'Collective Identities in a Changing
    Europe' in Martin McLoone (ed.), *Culture,Identity and Broadcasting in Ireland*
    (Belfast: Institute of Irish Studies, 1991) for some discussion of the place of
    Eastern Europe in the new European order.

2   Stuart Hall, 'Cultural Identity and Cinematic Representation' in *Framework*,
    no.36, 1989, p.70.

3   However, it should be noted that membership of the MEDIA programme
    has not been restricted to EC members. Five European Free Trade
    Association (EFTA) countries – Austria, Finland, Iceland, Norway and
    Sweden – joined in March 1993, Hungary joined in July 1993 and Poland
    joined the MEDIA line EFDO (European Film Distribution Office) in 1992.

4   *European Filmfile*, no. 4, vol.1, April 1993, pp.1–7.

5   Even a very minimal definition of a European film is not necessarily
    straightforward as *Screen Finance* has revealed in relation to EC directives and
    their interpretation by individual member states. See Nick Hobdell, 'Europe
    wrestles with burgeoning film definitions', *Screen Finance*, 3 November 1993,
    pp.9–11.

6   Writing in the 1960s, Alan Lovell suggests that there is a unity to European
    cinema based upon ' a sense that the cinema can be used as a medium for
    personal artistic creation ... (and) ... a feeling that the film-maker has a
    rightful place in the artistic tradition of his society'. See 'Introduction' in
    Alan Lovell (ed.) *Art of the Cinema in Ten European Countries* (Council for
    Cultural Co-operation: Strasbourg, 1967), p.19 ; also Steve Neale, 'Art
    Cinema as Institution' , *Screen*, vol. 22, no.1, 1981. The partial decline of the
    European art film during the 1980s and 1990s is discussed by Thomas
    Elsaesser, 'Chronicle of a Death Retold', *Monthly Film Bulletin*, June 1987,
    pp.164–67.

7   See 'Cinema and Their Audiences : Just Holding On', *Screen Digest*,
    September 1992, p. 205.

8   'Film Production : Signs of European recovery?', *Screen Digest*, April 1992,
    p.82; also 'European Film Production : Growth Potential Identified', *Screen
    Digest*, March 1991, p.60.

9   ibid., p.62.

10 See Matteo Maggiore, *Audiovisual Production in the Single Market*
    (Luxembourg : Commission of the European Communities, 1990), p.60.

11 Lawrence Cohn, 'Unbearable Lightness of Being in Foreign Film
    Production', *Variety*, 4 May 1988, pp. 59, 203–227.

12 Lloyd Shepherd, 'UK films get $150million at the US box-office', *Screen
    Finance*, 24 February 1993, pp. 6–10. It is also worth noting that the biggest
    success in 1992, *The Lawnmower Man*, was only marginally a 'British'
    production.

13 These figures and percentages are derived from calculations made by
    Goldman Sachs which appear in *Screen Finance*, 5 May 1993, p.8.

14 According to estimates in *Screen Digest*, video (both retail and rental)
    accounted for 41.1 per cent of European spending on film in 1992, cinema
    box-office accounted for 34.8 per cent and pay TV (on the basis of less than
    6% penetration of homes with television) accounted for 24.1 per cent. See
    'Spending on the Movies: The new media mix', *Screen Digest*, March 1993,
    pp.59–60.

15 Terry Ilott, 'UK Film, Television and Video : Statistical Overview', in *BFI Film and Television Yearbook 1993* (London : BFI, 1992), p.63.

16 'US penetration of Europe grows 50 per cent in 12 years', *Screen Finance*, 25 March 1992, pp. 14–15.

17 'Film Production : Signs of European recovery?', p.84.

18 'Hollywood increases its penetration of East Europe', *Screen Finance*, 3 June 1992, p.15.

19 'European Film Production', p. 64.

20 See London Economics, *Retailing European Films: The case of the European Exhibition Industry* (Madrid: Media Business School, 1993). UIP was granted an exemption from EC anti-competition rules in 1989 but this was up for review in 1993. See Nick Hobdell, 'UIP faces new EC competition debate as five-year exemption expires', *Screen Finance*, 30 June 1993, pp.1–3.

21 The expansion of US exhibition interests in Europe is discussed in 'European Cinema : Britain leads renaissance' in *Screen Digest* , August 1989, pp.177–184.

22 Steve Neale, 'Art Cinema as Institution', p.34. It is not entirely the case that Hollywood domination has always been perceived in national terms. Kristin Thompson discusses the emergence of the idea of 'Film Europe' in the 1920s in *Exporting Entertainment : America in the World Film Market 1907–1934* (London: BFI,1985).

23 ' Film Production : Signs of European Recovery?', pp.81–88.

24 *Screen Finance*, 5 May 1993, p. 9. What these figures also reveal is that while the studios continued to make more or less the same number of films during the 1980s (150 in 1982 and 157 in 1989) their average cost rose considerably (from $16.7 million to $32.7 million in the same period). The size of Hollywood budgets (and the large proportion spent on advertising and promotion) has, of course, tended to reinforce the competitive advantage of Hollywood in the world film market.

25 *Screen Finance*, 7 October 1992, p. 12. In 1992 the Hamburg Film Fund, one of the largest in Europe, also announced its intention to fund fewer, more expensive films. See *Screen International*, 10–16 July 1992, p. 5.

26 John Hopewell, 'Doing the Continental : A push for European Film', in *Moving Pictures International*, 28 January 1993, p.27.

27 British Screen Advisory Council, *The European Initiative : The Business of Film and Television in the 1990s* (London : BSAC, 1991), pp.4–5.

28 Jane Headland and Simon Relph, *The View from Downing Street* (London : BFI, 1991), p.21.

29 Coopers and Lybrand, *European Film : Industry or Art?* (London,1992).

30 Martin Dale, *Europa Europa : Developing the European Film Industry* (Academie Carat and Media Business School, 1992), p.93.

31 London Economics, *The Competitive Position of the European and US Film Industries* (Madrid : Media Business School, 1993), chap. 7.

32 Dale, *Europa Europa*, p.84.

33 Coopers and Lybrand, *European Film*, p. 8.

34 Dale, *Europa, Europa* , p.64.

35 See John Hopewell, *Professional Film and TV Production : Seminar Report* (Madrid : Media Business School, 1991), pp.31–2.

36 This is a point well made by John Tomlinson in *Cultural Imperialism* (London: Pinter, 1991).

37 See, for example, Soren Schou, 'Postwar Americanisation and the

revitalisation of European Culture' in Michael Skovmand and Kim Christian
Schrøder (eds.) *Media Cultures : Reappraising Transnational Media* (London :
Routledge, 1992).

38   The universal pretensions of the Enlightenment tradition have, of course,
been subject to considerable critique by both 'postmodern' and 'postcolonial'
theory. Agnes Heller and Ferenc Feher explicitly identify the 'end of the
European project' as one of the central goals of postmodernism: 'At some
point the time had to come when Europeans were bound to question the
project "Europe" as a whole; when they had to expose the false claim of
universalism inherent in the "European particular".' See Heller and Feher,
The Postmodern Political Condition (Cambridge : Polity Press, 1990), p.2.

39   Dale, *Europa,Europa* , p.93

40   See, for example, Kevin Robins, 'Reimagined Communities? European
Image Spaces, Beyond Fordism', *Cultural Studies*, vol.3, no. 2, 1989,
pp. 145–165.

41   Dale, *Europa,Europa*, p.1

42   Richard Dyer and Ginette Vincendeau, 'Introduction' in Dyer and
Vincendeau (eds.), *Popular European Cinema* (London : Routledge, 1992).

43   The evidence suggests that, unlike the cinema, European television
audiences maintain a preference for domestic programmes. According to
research by Television Business International, the average proportion of
European programming shown on the various national channels in Europe
was 68 per cent in 1989. See, Janet Watson (ed.), *Co-Production Europe*
(London:IPPA, 1990), p.1.

44   Ien Ang, 'Hegemony-in-Trouble : Nostalgia and the Ideology of the
Impossible in European Cinema' in Duncan Petrie (ed.), *Screening Europe :
Image and Identity in Contemporary European Cinema* (London : BFI, 1992),
p.28.

45   Terry Ilott, 'What Europe Really Needs', *Impact*, no.5, August 1992, p. 23.

46   According to figures in *Screen Digest*, there are three European companies –
Philips (Polygram), Italy's Fininvest and Germany's Bertelsmann – amongst
the leading top ten audio-visual companies in the world as measured by
turnover. See 'The World's Top AV Companies', *Screen Digest*, August 1993,
pp.181–184.

47   Ian Christie,'National Cultural Identity in Television and Film – European
Methods of Subsidising National Production and Protection Against
Multinational Penetration', in *The European Film in the World Market* (Austrian
Film Commission, 1989), p.17.

48   *MEDIA : Guide for the Audiovisual Industry* (Brussels : Commission of the
European Communities, 1992), Edition 8, p.3.

49   Dale, *Europa,Europa*, p. 47.

50   *MEDIA : Guide*, p.3. For a summary of the projects supported by MEDIA, see
the appendix to Paul Hainsworth's chapter in this volume.

51   'Film Production : Signs of European Recovery?', p.82.The definition of a
co-production being employed here is a generous one and includes both
'official' co-productions made under inter-government treaties (in order to
take advantage of national forms of support) and 'unofficial' ones; it also
includes a variety of co-production arrangements (including co-financing
and pre-selling). For an overview of co-production arrangements, see Janet
Watson (ed.), *Co-Production Europe.*

52   *Screen Finance*, 11 August 1993, p. 11.

53 Edward Buscombe, 'Nationhood, Culture and Media Boundaries : Britain' in *Quarterly Review of Film and Video*, vol. 14, no. 3, 1993, p. 30.

54 For an overview of these attempts see Robert Murphy, 'Under the Shadow of Hollywood' in Charles Barr (ed.), *All Our Yesterdays : 90 Years of British Cinema* (London :BFI, 1986), pp.47–69.

55 While *Howards End* was the most financially successful British film of 1992 it was still only 35th in the UK box-office ranking for the year. As for *Enchanted April*, its box-office performance was insufficient for it to figure in the top 150 for 1991 and by the time of the Oscar nominations it had already been shown, without ceremony, on television as part of the BBC's *Screen Two* series.

56 Mark Le Fanu and Neil McCartney, 'Troubled Working Party Report Unlikely To Be Ready Before Autumn', *Screen Finance*, 12 June 1991, p.2.

57 Wilf Stevenson, 'Preface', in Headland and Relph, *The View From Downing Street*, p.viii. The idea of Britain as the 'Hollywood of Europe' has been continued in the sixth volume to appear in the *UK Film Initiatives* series : Geoff Mulgan and Richard Paterson (eds.) *Hollywood of Europe : The Future of British Film* (London : BFI, 1993).

58 Dale, *Europa,Europa*, p.45.

59 Ben Gibson, 'Unpack the Pudding', *Impact*, no.5, October 1992, p. 16.

60 For a review of these developments see John Hill, 'Government Policy and the British Film Industry 1979-90', *European Journal of Communication*, vol.8, no.2, 1993, pp.203–24.

61 'State Film Aid Schemes', *Screen Digest*, July 1984, p.127. The differences in national funding of film within Europe are summarised in Patricia Perilli (ed.), *A Level Playing Field?* (London : BFI, 1991).

62 The UK officially joined Eurimages on 1 April 1993 after a three-month period of informal membership. Peter Greenaway's *Prospero's Books* (1991) had previously received support from Eurimages but this was because of the involvement of co-production partners from three member states (France, Italy and the Netherlands).The first majority-UK co-production to receive support was the the Anglo/French documentary *Tales From A Hard City* and the first majority-UK feature (with Italian and Swiss partners) was, *In the Hollow of the Deep Sea Wave* .

63 Terry Ilott, 'Failure in USA stokes enthusiasm for Europe', *Screen Finance*, 6 September 1990, p.9.

64 The European Co-production Fund (ECF) was set up in 1991 as a subsidiary of British Screen Finance on an initial budget of £5 million over three years. By 1993 six ECF-backed films had been completed, including *Orlando* (1993), *The Cement Garden* (1993) and *Damage* (1993), and a further seven had gone into production, including a French co-production, *Le Roi de Paris* and the Irish/German/Dutch co-production, *Rosaril.* The European Co-production Fund has been instrumental in increasing the money coming from Europe into UK production and, in 1992, EC sources provided 31 per cent of British Screen's total investment in film, compared with only 3 per cent in 1989. See Lloyd Shepherd and Neil McCartney, 'EC raises 30 per cent finance for BSF films', *Screen Finance*, 6 October 1993, pp.1, 12–16.

65 Ben Gibson, 'Seven Deadly Myths', in Duncan Petrie (ed.), *New Questions of British Cinema* (London : BFI, 1992), p.32. Gibson is head of BFI Production which has increasingly orientated itself towards Europe. See 'BFI Takes European Co-Production Route', *Screen Finance*, 12 August 1992, pp.13–16.

66   Oscar Moore, 'UK Preview 1992', *Screen International,* 24 January 1992, p. 13.
     The dangers of too self-consciously a European approach are illustrated by
     one of Ken Loach's films prior to *Riff-Raff,* the UK/German/French
     co-production *Fatherland* (1986) which awkwardly links together its German
     and British plot-lines and lacks the sense of a specific social milieu
     characteristic of Loach's best work.
67   See John Hill, 'The Issue of National Cinema and British Film Production'
     in Petrie (ed.), *New Questions of British Cinema,* pp. 10–21.

CREATIVITY AND COMMERCIALISM :
FILM-MAKING IN EUROPE

David Puttnam

As I write this I am on location with my latest production *War of the Buttons* (1994). It's being filmed entirely in west Cork, with an all-Irish cast. Does that make it an Irish film, I ask myself, conscious of the fact that the tax-man, for one, will be particularly interested in my answer? Fortunately, as a consequence of the 1993 Finance Act, the Irish government has made that a simple question with a very simple and entirely logical answer, at least so far as tax arrangements are concerned. But in other respects, the answer is less straightforward. The script is by an English writer, based on a French novel with French and British as well as Irish money invested. So, can I at least call it a 'European' film? Well, not quite, because it's also attracted American and Japanese distribution investment.

In the far south west of Ireland – about as close as a European can get to Hollywood without getting his or her feet wet – the distinctions between European and American cinema begin to feel more than a little abstract. My concern at the moment is simply to make a successful film – a film that reaches out to its audience but also a film that has something worth reaching them with. Forget about it origins and its parentage! Here in west Cork we are attempting to combine those qualities which for me typify the best of American cinema – narrative drive, energy, acccessibility – with the best of what European cinema has to offer – the kind of subtlety and sophistication which the mainstream Hollywood product so rarely seems to capture. That fusion of the best of American cinema with the finest European sensibilities is something I've striven to achieve throughout my career as a producer – not always with total success! That doesn't make me unique. Any serious filmmaker knows that the desire to make lasting works of art must be balanced against the need – even the

81

desire – to make a living. Indeed, the tension between creativity and commercial necessity is the life-blood of our industry and yet so often we resist acknowledging that simple fact.

In Europe we jealously guard the purity of the creative process from what we ignorantly parody as the crude commercialism of the Hollywood majors, ignoring some of the glaringly obvious lessons which the Hollywood industry offers to other less consistently successful film industries, such as ours. In fairness, Hollywood, too, finds it hard to learn, an attitude epitomised many years ago by Billy Wilder's scornful instruction to one of his cameramen to 'shoot a few scenes out of focus so you can win a foreign film award'.

Perhaps perversely, I've found that the projects that have attracted me as sure-fire commercial winners have frequently been the ones that are impossible to push to a successful conclusion, whereas those to which I am drawn by some dream-like, magical quality – however indefinable that may be and however prolonged and painful the project's development – are the ones that ultimately succeed. The lesson is obvious: the central story has to be something towards which I feel a passionate commitment and it must be a story which has the potential to reach out and influence a broad and diverse audience. There are plenty of passionately committed film-makers in Europe. The question we have to address remains very basic – is there an audience for the films we want to make?

What's certain is that no-one can predict the combination of ingredients that will bring success. That's part of the 'magic' and it always will be. But in the face of what is a real crisis in European film-making, perhaps the time has come to be a little more attuned to the legitimate and consistent appetite of our audience. There is, after all, a huge and growing audience. We ought not to let rapidly developing technology and changing social habits obscure the fact that more people are watching more movies than ever before. Yet for all the growth and change, the European film industry is at an historic low point, average budgets have actually declined in recent years and what is in its very essence a mass medium is in danger of being served by little more than a cottage industry. A recent analysis suggested that more than 60 per cent of the films produced in Germany are seen by fewer than 20,000 people!

In 1992 the European Community ran an audio-visual trade deficit with the United States of $3.5 billion, and that figure is very likely to go on growing in the years ahead. In the case of Britain, a trade surplus with the United States of £24 million a year in television programmes in 1985 had, by 1991, become a deficit of £100 million and is forecast to be £640 million by the end of the decade. The economic consequences are bad enough; the price to be paid in terms of Europe's cultural vitality is even greater. It's not as if European cinema is devoid of talent. Quite the reverse. It has provided and continues to provide a reservoir that constantly refreshes the Hollywood industry, both technically and artistically – so much that part of our wider responsibility as film-makers must be to keep nurturing that talent and the cultural values that produce it. The point is that for all our evident ability to generate talent it seems that we are a good deal less capable of generating success or – to be really blunt about it – money. When it opened in the United States in the summer of 1993, *Jurassic Park* (1993) was taking as much money every week-end as the British government invests in British cinema – archives, training, production funds, the British Film Institute – in the course of a whole year.

What are the lessons we can learn? The first, and perhaps most compelling lesson, is that the Americans see their industry as a totality. They recognise that an 'industry' is not simply a manufacturing process – whether it's cars, or food or movies. It's a series of connected activities – production, distribution, marketing and so on – all of which are important, all of which are mutually dependent. The marketing budget for *Jurassic Park* exceeded its production budget – and the studio is collecting a handsome reward on both investments. At the other extreme, the UK promotion budget of the *The Crying Game* (1992) was £50,000 and, sadly, it paid the price at the UK box-office. In the United States, however, it has done more than $60 million worth of business for its courageous distributor. In Britain the recent and welcome growth in box-office is nearly all accounted for by the multiplex cinemas and it's no accident that the vast majority of them are built, owned and run by American companies. They had the foresight to develop the novel idea that if you make a cinema somewhere attractive and welcoming, then people will flock to it.

In Britain we have allowed all our concern, certainly our media concern, to centre on one part of the industry – production – largely ignoring changes to the distribution and exhibition networks which could put more British films on British screens, increasing the likelihood of some of them achieving box-office success. France, the country with the most thriving film industry in Europe, re-cycles money within the industry, using some of it to build and modernise cinemas, and ensure that adequate numbers of prints are available of new French films. The result is there are two and a half times as many screens as in Britain for a population that is roughly the same and, coincidentally, two and a half times as many domestically produced films, in percentage terms, on television.

The French system does not depend on huge amounts of state support but by re-cycling money, by offering tax-breaks and intelligent incentives, it has helped to generate and sustain a relatively dynamic industry. I calculated recently that were we to adopt a similar network of support in Britain we could generate almost £250 million of additional investment for film production alone, at an additional cost to the tax-payer of less than £2 million. Repeated across the European Community this could stimulate about £1 billion in production finance, radically altering the scale, quantity and range of European film production. We would be doubling the number of films we make in Europe and, perhaps as importantly in the midst of economic recession, doubling employment in the industry. To those who dismiss such a scenario as the kind of fantasy only a film-maker could entertain, I reply with one word – Airbus. Twenty years ago three US manufacturers completely dominated the world aircraft industry. Today the European Airbus is in second place, with 28% of the world market, and is at the cutting edge of new technology in flight control systems. It can be done.

The success of Airbus lay not in imitating the American manufacturers but in very deliberately setting out to plan and develop an entirely new range of aircraft. Similarly, I'm not suggesting that the way for European film-makers to succeed is by re-cycling someone else's tired old formulas, or attempting to make third-rate imitations of successful American movies. The most successful examples of European cinema have always been rooted in the specific: Fellini's world couldn't have been more specific, and audiences everywhere were able to identify with the emotions, hopes and dreams of his characters. In Europe today, directors such as Almodovar are to an extent doing the same thing – and frequently achieving success, both artistically and commercially. One of the most marvellous examples in recent years of a culturally specific film which reached out to millions of people outside its own country was Lasse Hallström's *My Life as a Dog* (1985). It was funny, touching, and stuffed full of energy and life – those same universal qualities which, sadly, seem so often to be missing from contemporary European movies.

Of course, this desire to reach out to an audience is only one issue facing European film-makers – but it's the one over which we have at least some control. In contrast, the increasingly restrictive distribution system is a commercial reality over which it is hard for individual film-makers to feel they have any influence at all. I do believe there is a strong case for some form of 'constructive intervention' from European governments to encourage exhibitors, and television broadcasters, to show European movies and, in so doing, help sustain some kind of European identity. I hasten to add that does not mean I am in favour of widespread subsidies to prop up work which, left to it's own devices, would never find an audience. Like any other performance-enhancing drug, the first and only rule with subsidies is that they should be used very sparingly and under strict supervision!

The same applies to production. Subsidies to redress the huge imbalance of a market-place dominated by American cinema will always be on the agenda. But they must be carefully targeted and directed in a culturally specific manner. It's probably true to say that the low-budget end of European production – around five or six million dollars – is an area in which we struggle along quite adequately. It remains possible to recoup costs, even in a worldwide market-place within which the audience for sub-titled films is constantly falling. But if our ambitions encourage us to make films with budgets above that figure, then we run into problems. It's very hard for a purely European film costing ten or twelve million dollars to recoup its cost unless it has either the backing of a Hollywood major to guarantee worldwide distribution or some other 'commercial element' which will help it in the international market-place.

This all adds up to a rather depressing scenario and poses a question to which I don't pretend to have an answer, namely, how do we in Europe fit our creative dreams into the budget limitations which the market-place seems to impose on us? I return again to the central elements of any film – its story and its characters. If these do connect with an audience, if the director is able to realise his or her dream with genuine style and flair then, ultimately, large budgets and star names become secondary. That being true, and given the potential size of our European market, it must remain possible to look within Europe for funding rather than gaze longingly towards the richer and apparently easier shores of the United States. I take great heart from the fact that a film like *Toto the Hero* (1991) was financed entirely from European sources. It was an ambitious piece of work, made on a tight budget raised from a multitude of countries and sources – a salutary example of what can be achieved by tenacity and confidence.

My sense is that European cinema has not yet come to terms with the realities of life in an age of television and, more specifically, pay-cable and satellite. Every single British Oscar nomination last year was substantially dependent on television finance and backing. Already the video rental and sell-through market is more than double traditional box-office earnings. In the US the whole industry is to a very large extent underpinned by deals with the domestic pay-cable companies and as entertainment corporations combine or slug it out with telecom corporations to extend the million of miles of fibre-optic cable, the relationship is bound to get even closer. It's my belief that within ten years pay-cable could account for between 60 and 70 per cent of total revenues. That means taking our relationship with the cable operators very seriously indeed so that we can create a proper partnership, not a grossly unbalanced market in which all creativity has been surrendered to the power of distribution company accountants.

We are not powerless victims. The video, cable and satellite operators all know that at the end of the day they feed off a dynamic film industry, not the other way round. Indeed, in Britain, while the overall audience for film continues to grow, the overall audience for television is, if anything, beginning to decline. We all want to see a flourishing film production industry in Europe. I certainly want Britain to win back a place as a significant maker of films. But I'm not interested in defining European success in terms of American defeat. There's room for everybody. At present its true to say that the cake is divided unevenly, but it's a very big cake and there are many dense and rich layers to it. What must concern us all is the balance of ingredients going into that cake. I continue to believe that there is a quality in European film-making which is unique. That's the strength we draw on, and it's my abiding belief that by exploring the fusion of American and European cinema, or by exploiting the potential of a combination of creative and commercial energy, we extend rather than diminish the quality of production. That makes the whole of our industry – and the wider economy – real beneficiaries. Most important of all, our audiences benefit too. That's what really matters. Our concern must be to produce films that move, entertain and inspire people – that speak to them wherever they are in the world.

VANISHING POINT :
Feature Film Production in a Small Country

Steve McIntyre

Introduction

This paper started life as part of a report to the Scottish Screen Industry Project, of which the author was the Director. It seems appropriate, therefore, to begin with a brief comment on this project and the context within which it emerged. As a broad research and development undertaking which attempted to identify mechanisms and strategies to expand the screen industry (across the board) in Scotland, it (somewhat inadvertently) stood at the end of a long line of similar 'cultural industries' initiatives that sprang up across the UK in the mid- and late-1980s. From Sheffield's Media Industries Quarter to Birmingham's Media Development Agency and from the North East Media Development Association to Cardiff Media City, the cry went out: 'invest in these industries not (just) because they are culturally significant but because they are global growth areas and will generate inward investment, jobs and urban regeneration'. Moreover, it was argued, they have a clean and modern image which, it was believed, might smooth the process of other, unrelated company relocation into regions and cities suffering from the collapse of their heavy industry base. As to cultural outcomes – well that would be an added bonus.

The history of this rash of cultural industries developments – of the shifts and re-directions of the arguments, of the increasing attenuation of the first half of the culture/industry couplet, and of their success or failure (on whatever grounds) – still has to be written. Even without an adequate, comprehensive chart of this process, it is still possible to identify a couple of the specific inflections that distinguished the Scottish Screen Industry Project from other media development schemes in the English regions.

First was the almost complete evacuation of cultural concern. Funded by Scottish Enterprise (the Scottish development agency), the Scottish Screen Industry Project was *only* to deal with questions of employment, economic growth and the like. As such, it stood shoulder to shoulder with promotion of the electronics industry, tourism or Scotch Whisky. Second, and of course in massive contradiction with the first point, the project also carried the weight of desire to create a national feature film industry. This partly derived from a fairly predictable national ambition to play on the world stage but it also expressed more creditable imperatives concerned with national self-expression and the interrogation of questions of national identity.

This paper attempts to examine only one part of this cluster of issues – the possibility of a feature film industry in a small country. In passing, however, I just want to offer a couple of brief comments about the wisdom of treating the cultural industries *only* as industries and relying exclusively on industrial strategies derived from, say, manufacturing industry, in order to foster growth. Certainly a concern for investment criteria, for business skills training, for market specialisation and for internationalism are all important but they do not get to the heart of things. In Scotland, the screen industries are overwhelmingly the broadcasters: Scottish Television, Grampian, Border Television and BBC Scotland make up about 90 per cent of the £300m per annum industry. The world of broadcasting in the UK is both deeply London-biased and heavily regulated politically – it is not a geographically neutral, free market. In order to have any chance of intervening successfully in this arena, any development strategy must recognise and face up to these factors. Addressing the commanding heights of the screen industries relies on effective utilisation of social, cultural and political arguments – of Scotland's right to self-expression and of the responsibility of national broadcasting institutions and structures to reflect properly the complexity and diversity of the UK as a whole, rather than only that world inside the M25. Using these arguments, real gains might be made. Winning the political and cultural case for networked drama, current affairs, light entertainment and so on, which speak with a Scottish voice, will have a much more profound impact on the Scottish screen industry *qua* industry than any amount of expansion of its ability to produce training videos. A precedent exists in the successful lobbying undertaken (on, of course, linguistic and social terms) to establish the £10 million per annum Gaelic Television Fund as a consequence of which a thriving Gaelic language production industry has now been forged. In other words, developing the Scottish screen industries means making the cultural and political case to defend and expand the work of BBC Scotland, it means building a case for 'fair shares of the network', it means standing up for a networked *Take the High Road*... The culture/industry hybrid is complex and paradoxical. After more than a decade when emphasis has increasingly rested upon questions of jobs, investment, economic growth and the like (with 'culture' as an accidental by-product) is there not a certain pleasure to be derived from a recognition that industrial development in the regions and national regions of the UK might in fact depend upon a robust and unembarrassed presentation of the cultural case?

The focus of this paper, however, is the possibility of expanding and developing the range of indigenous feature (theatrically released) films made in, for and from Scotland. The focus here is mainly on an analysis of the economics of film-making, rather than on cultural concern, although the two do need to be brought together in any fully adequate consideration of what kind of film-making might be possible in Scotland. For the most part, this paper treats Scottish film-making as a sub-set of British, which in turn is a sub-set of European, film-making. This is because of Scotland's position within the legislative and financial context of the British film industry and Britain's position, in common with the rest of Europe, vis-à-vis the structural competitive advantage of Hollywood. In other words, while France, for example, makes two or three times the number of films that Britain does, this is for reasons of language and subsidy. Its industrial competitive disadvantage compared with Hollywood is exactly the same as Britain. The big picture is necessary to understand the specific position of Scotland which is dealt with at the end of this section. Because of this, I have not attempted to 'generalise' the arguments. The same analysis that is offered can be made *mutatis mutandis* for Wales and Ireland.

An assumption is made in most of the following that there will be no significant change to the operating climate for British film-making. In actual fact, this may not be the case and the circumstances of the British film industry may alter. It is my contention, however, that the structural disadvantage of the

European industry is such that even significant modifications to the fiscal operating climate in the UK will not create an industry that can compete on equal terms with Hollywood. Certainly, more films may be made (and that is, of course, welcome) but that is not the same thing as creating an internationally competitive industry.

Clearing the Ground
In order to focus the analysis properly, there is an urgent need to kill off a few sacred cows and abandon the loose talk and idle dreaming that often characterise discussion of Scottish or British feature film production (or, rather, the lack of it). Unpleasant at it might be, it is necessary to recognise that:

1.   Developing a Scottish feature film industry could never be a case of simply persuading corporate and institutional financiers that this is a real, immediate business opportunity. Financiers are not stupid: if there were real, immediate, financial opportunities, is it not likely that they would have grasped them? As will be seen, however, a judicious mix of public and private money, invested on varying terms, might attract financial interest.
2.   There are few, if any, significant cost or other benefits accruing to film-making in Scotland. While certain costs are arguably lower, this is offset by absences like studios, labs, and the like and by uncertain weather. If film-makers are looking for a real bargain basement they will, for the immediate future, think about Eastern Europe.
3.   The competitive advantage of the Hollywood film machine is so overwhelming that a Scottish (or British) film industry will not emerge simply by the elimination of a few structural blockages to allow Scottish (or British) film-making to flourish.
4.   A question mark must exist as to whether there currently exists the talent and skills in or from Scotland to build such an industry.
5.   Vague arguments about 'critical mass' (e.g. that ten feature films a year would spread costs, maximise returns and thereby establish an ongoing secure industry in Scotland) usually tend to obscure rather than illuminate the facts of the case.
6.   Questions about what kind of film-making can be undertaken in Scotland are central to any consideration of this issue.
7. The role of Scottish cinema exhibition in enabling a film production industry is financially insignificant.

With this Gradgrindish exercise in blunt reality complete, it is now possible to turn to the key features of the international and national movie making scene in order to establish what kinds of film-making might be possible in Scotland, and what the financial basis of this might be.

Money no Object

One key mistake usually made when thinking about film production is to focus on the difficulty of raising the actual production money. This is often considered to be a problem with the financial institutions and the financial markets : if only they could see the opportunities they are being offered and take advantage of them, everything would be all right. A recent report from London Economics asks whether the problem is really the supply of finance:

> It could be argued that the market has demonstrated its efficiency at weeding out the poor projects, and financing those with good prospects. This a priori view is supported by casual empirical evidence. European bankers assert that their problem is in finding credible European films to finance, rather than any innate conservatism on their part. The success of European films relative to American supported ones, goes some way to supporting this view. The willingness of European banks to be players in Hollywood again provides evidence for the view that the banks do not have a natural resistance to film per se.[1]

The problem, therefore, is likely to be on the demand side, not the supply side of finance. There are simply inadequate numbers of projects which are structured, as far as financial institutions are concerned, so as to have sufficient earning potential to cover their costs. Those banks (such as Guinness Mahon, Crédit Lyonnais) that do participate in lending to film projects make, it is reported, a handsome profit on this business. Under normal circumstances, they share very little of the risk that the film will fail – that is usually carried by distributors who underwrite the film by way of pre-sales. In other words, there is little evidence that a properly structured film project (with adequate pre-sales and identified income streams) will have difficulty raising finance. The difficulty of so structuring a film project in the UK (or, more specifically, in Scotland) is another, and more difficult, question.

Hooray for Hollywood

Financial institutions are geographically neutral (i.e. they will, all other things being equal, as readily lend to a production in Scotland as Los Angeles). Why, therefore, is the latter market a magnet for finance – what is the competitive advantage of the Hollywood film industry? Reflect, for a moment, on William Goldman's immortal assessment of the dynamics of the movie business – 'Nobody knows anything!'.[2] In other words, nobody, from the highest studio head to the studio gofer knows what films are going to work, what films are going to make money and what films are going to close studios. While *Batman Returns* (1992) might be a pretty good bet, who can predict (apart from with hindsight) the reception of a *Hudson Hawk* (1991), an *Ishtar* (1987), or a *Ghost* (1990) and *Pretty Woman* (1990)? Closer to home, why *My Beautiful Laundrette* (1985) and not *London Kills Me* (1991), why *A Letter to Brezhnev* (1985) and not *Blonde Fist* (1991)? Or, even closer, why *Gregory's Girl* (1980) and not *The Girl in the Picture* (1985)? And so on. The point of this is that each film is unique – the movie business is a prototype industry. Each time it brings together a unique combination of elements (script, financial package, actors, etc.), never knowing, for sure, what the finished product will look like and how the eventual film will be received.

As a mature industry, Hollywood has, of course, evolved a number of mechanisms to attempt to overcome, as far as possible, this serious problem of massive future uncertainty. It attempts to replicate elements of proven successes in order to guarantee future successes. Some of these elements might be :
– use of stars
– use of known talent (especially writers, directors and producers)
– use of special effects
– sequels
– generic labelling
What is significant about this list is that none of these characteristics could be readily attached to British film-making.

Hollywood also employs a number of strategies to create a 'must see' feeling around a film:
– massive advertising and promotional campaigns
– platform releases
– massive trailering
– previews to create word of mouth

– early exploitation of ancillary markets (toys, games, tee-shirts, etc.)

Again, with a few notable exceptions, such strategies are not employed to promote British films (either at home or abroad) – for good reason.

What can be discerned beneath both lists is money: it is axiomatic in Hollywood that the more that is spent on a film the more likely it is to make a serious return. That is, a $20 million movie with possibly another $10 million spent on a platform US release is a better commercial risk than a $5 million independent production. And nobody is going to risk a lot of promotional money on a low-budget movie that doesn't have the known (expensive) talent base which at least gives it a fighting chance in the mass market-place (i.e. it enables the film 'to open'). Now, in order to spread risks as much as possible, a serious player in the game is not going to make one $20 million film but ten or twenty. It will be necessary, therefore, to have access to the widest range of talent, to the biggest stars, to the best ideas, to the most skilled 'deal-makers' and agents, and so on. In other words it will be necessary to trade in and with Hollywood. It is significant, in this regard, that the huge investment in film production from Japanese companies (e.g. Sony, Matsushita, Pioneer) has been by way of exploiting the Hollywood market (acquisition and investment in US companies) rather than by attempting to compete.[3]

Another key element of Hollywood's pre-eminence is distribution. It is difficult to overestimate the centrality of this to the financial muscle of Hollywood. In order to be able to service the huge costs of a slate of major films, buy in the necessary talent and fund project development, the income from distribution is crucial. The major studios in the US (Warner Bros., Buena Vista/ Disney, MCA/Universal, Paramount, Fox) dominate the US movie business because they control the means of distribution. Even though independent production companies produce more films than these five, the majors earned 70 per cent of the US box-office returns in 1990. A recent study by Robins and Aksoy concluded that:

> Financial muscle is acquired through controlling the distribu-
> tion stage where the money is made in rentals from cinemas
> and new media outlets across the world. The Hollywood studios

owe their long standing position in the film industry to their strategy of controlling the critical hubs in the film business, that is, distribution and finance.[4]

The US majors control distribution not only at home but also in all major markets overseas. Two thirds of UK distribution is accounted for by just two companies – UIP and Warner Brothers – which are, in turn, controlled by five of the seven top US studios. Box-office returns (in economists' jargon, rents), therefore, return to what is already the centre, that is Hollywood (although, from there, they might well be repatriated to Japan).

Another feature of Hollywood production is its immense skill in producing movies for the single largest audience segment: the 12-29 year olds. More than 60 per cent of the global audience for cinema comes from this age group. Given that the US market is approximately 50 per cent of the global market for what might best be called 'western cinema', it is clear that there is a massive home audience for the bulk of Hollywood's output: 30 per cent of the total global cinema audience is made up of American 12-29 year olds. Hollywood has *the* most lucrative primary cinema market segment on its doorstep. It can, therefore, in the main, make a profit in home territories, with overseas sales as icing on the cake. And, certainly, an additional 30 per cent of world audiences made up of 12-29 year olds in Europe, Japan, Canada and Australia, with tastes, in the main, dominated by American cinema, comprise very lucrative secondary markets.[5]

The Competitive (Dis)Advantage of Nations

Hollywood dominates the world's cinema industry because it is the 'thickest market'. In exactly the same way that a new restaurant will be wise to open in a part of town already characterised as an eating-out spot, or a new financial services operation will trade in the City of London, so too in the film industry the tendency will always be for trade to gravitate to the market which is already the strongest. Another way of putting this is that in the thickest market there will 'cluster' the widest choice of every conceivable element necessary to the complex process of putting together a movie. At every stage of this process, therefore, high quality, competitively-priced services will be available. The compass of movie finance, therefore, inevitably points in this direction.

The business guru Michael Porter's monumental study on the condition of world business, *The Competitive Advantage of Nations*, identifies clustering of primary, secondary and related industries as a key element in business advantage: in building and sustaining industrial energy and innovation and in maintaining barriers to entry to other national industries:

> One competitive industry helps to create another in a mutually reinforcing process. Such an industry is often the most sophisticated buyer of the products and services it depends on. Its presence in a nation becomes important to developing competitive advantage in supplier industries ... Competitive supplier industries in a nation also help encourage world-class downstream industries. They provide technology, stimulate transferable factor creation, and become new entrants. One internationally competitive industry also creates new related industries, through providing ready access to transferable skills, through related entry by already established firms, or by stimulating entry indirectly through spin offs. Once a cluster forms, the whole group of industries becomes mutually supporting. Benefits flow forward, backward, and horizontally. Aggressive rivalry in one industry tends to spread to others in the cluster, through the exercise of bargaining power, spin-offs, and related diversification by established firms. Entry from other industries within the cluster spurs upgrading by stimulating diversity in R&D approaches and providing a means for introducing new strategies and skills ... The cluster becomes a vehicle for maintaining diversity and overcoming the inward focus, inertia, inflexibility and accommodation among rivals that slows or blocks competitive upgrading and new entry. The presence of the cluster helps increase information flow, the likelihood of new approaches, and new entry from spin-offs, downstream, upstream and related industries. It plays, in a sense, the role of creating "outsiders" from within the nation that will compete in new ways. National industries are thus able to sustain advantage instead of losing it to other nations who innovate.[6]

It is clear from the above analysis that Hollywood enjoys a massive clustering advantage: inevitably the talent, the deal makers, the cash, the financial services, the studio bosses, the distributors, the knowledge gatherers, the market makers, the publicity machines congregate here. And each deal that is done, each movie made, each fortune won or lost, and each shift in public taste reinforces this concentration. It is more than a simple critical mass of production undertaken, but a focus for all the central and ancillary operations necessary to maintain an overwhelmingly dominant position in global mainstream cinema.

William Goldman, in his idiosyncratic way, makes a similar point about the authority of Hollywood: you need to be in Los Angeles to pick up the 'word' on films, and on their probable reception, well before they even open in order to have half a chance of chasing the whims of public taste and therefore of planning future production strategies. Living in New York, London or Glasgow puts a film-maker months out of touch. Using the example of surprise smash hit *Porky's* (1981), he observes:

> Simply put, they know things out there that the rest of the country doesn't, and they get that information first. The movie business is part of the fabric of life in Los Angeles , and that just isn't true anywhere else. It is, if you will, in the air . . . And you better bet that before *Porky's* opened, every studio had at least two *Porky's* rip-offs in development. And when *Porky's II* opens – believe me, there will be a *Porky's II* – it will have been preceded by maybe three or four similar films.[7]

In other words, if you weren't living and working in Hollywood you would have missed out altogether on the opportunity of cashing in on a major business trend. Whatever the merits of demerits of *Porky's* as a film, the example is not facile (many other examples could be given). Hollywood and Hollywood alone, has its collective finger on the pulse (one pulse at least) of public taste and has the machinery in place to respond rapidly and exploit it.

Is it possible to construct an alternative movie industry cluster to rival Hollywood? Three options might present themselves. First would be massive financial incentives to induce enough market makers to relocate. This must be considered, to say the least, highly unlikely.

Second is the proposal, in some ways at the heart of the MEDIA programme, of creating a pan-European industry and a pan-European market.[8] If, however, the arguments made above about operational and spatial clustering are accepted, such a pan-continental industry would require concentration in one principal location and probably convergence on one language. This language might be English as this is, thanks to Hollywood, the one language, apart from its own, to which each European country is accustomed. On the other hand, another language might need to be used to by-pass the irresistible gravitational pull of Hollywood if English were to be used. The inherent implausibility of, say, France or Italy, abandoning the cultural and linguistic ambitions of their national cinemas need not be spelled out.

Third, is the possibility of creating a non-American, English language market-place. The English Language Cinema Plan (ELCP), an initiative currently being pushed by producers and state agencies in the UK, Ireland, Australia, New Zealand and Canada, is just such an attempt to forge an English-language economic area. While this effort to invent a new concept of 'home market', and to promote non-US English co-productions, might have a modest effect in increasing box-office returns and enabling more films to be made, it will do so within a (very) geographically dispersed context. It cannot create a rival centre of gravity to take on Hollywood. In other words, valuable as the ELCP and MEDIA are, they are unlikely to shift radically the international framework within which British (or European) films get made.

Two views of British cinema

Two broad approaches characterise discussion of British (or, indeed, European) cinema. The first of these might be called the 'blame the film-maker' school of thought. According to this line, if only British film-makers stopped contemplating their navels and started making films which audiences wanted to see, everything would be all right. According to this position, and there is some superficial evidence for it, British film-makers tend too much to go for the art house audience rather than produce crowd pleasers. There are, it is argued, too many film-makers like Ken Loach, Terence Davies and Peter Greenaway around, and they tend to define the nature of British cinema. In a broader European frame, of course, the *cinema d'auteur* reigns supreme. While British cinema can manage an occasional *Shirley Valentine* (1989), *A Fish Called Wanda* (1988), *Local Hero* (1983) or, more recently, *The Commitments* (1991), it makes nowhere near enough of these kinds of films.

Developing this theme recently, writer and commentator Terry Illot compares the risk-taking, market-driven cinema of

Hollywood and its clear audience appeal with the inward-looking, risk-averse cinema of Europe:

> With few exceptions (most of them working in Hollywood), European producers, directors and writers have lost confidence in their product. The aim now is not so much to win audiences as to win pre-sales, transferring as much of the risk as possible to distributors.[9]

The other position, represented by, for example, the Downing Street working parties of a few years back, and, unsurprisingly, most film-makers, emphasises structural and financial problems blocking the development of an indigenous film industry. Against this background, it is argued, British film-makers show considerable ingenuity and entrepreneurial energy in getting films made at all. Given a little more support and some kind of protection from the overwhelming power of Hollywood, the British industry could really take off.

As always in these kinds of arguments, there is some validity in both sides. If the analysis of Hollywood's ascendancy, developed above, is broadly accepted then it seems fundamentally unlikely that British and European film-makers can take on the US industry on its own terms : the large-budget mainstream film. The competitive advantage of the Hollywood industry is such that financiers will, quite correctly, always recognise it as the most plausible, profitable locus of film-making and make investment decisions accordingly. This is a perfectly rational business decision and, while it might grieve European film-makers to recognise it, it reflects little more than the effective operation of the market-place. In other words, no amount of native wit, creativity and endeavour will enable British film-makers effectively to compete directly with America – the market has failed Britain and will continue to do so.

This might suggest that rather than representing a retreat from the imperatives of the market-place, the sorts of specialised films that are produced across Europe reflect a rational choice. London Economics floats the following hypothesis:

> [Possibly] Europeans have confined themselves to the niches they currently serve precisely because they have no competitive advantage in the markets that LA dominates . . . There may be

little point in competing with LA head-on ... The competitive advantages in the art-house market are very different from those in the mass market. It is easier to have one-off, or sporadic, successes in the art-house sector. The need for a single distributor to feed a pipeline of films is reduced. The need to have a co-ordinated release pattern is reduced, because audience discrimination is more sophisticated. There are a smaller number of theatres to be co-ordinated anyway. Moreover, the lower budget films are easier to organise than large budget films and so, if Europe has a disadvantage in the organisation of inputs, then it will have less of a disadvantage here. The Europeans also have a strong advantage over LA in making films for their own domestic audiences.[10]

While in broad European terms, this argument has considerable force (think of the successful French film industry at home – even if it is a very highly subsidised one) it is much less convincing when applied to the British situation. If it were the case, why the continual talk of crisis? And why are so few films produced each year? Perhaps, after all, there is something in the 'blame the film-maker' school of thought and some kind of radical review of what kinds of films are made in Britain needs to be undertaken.

British Film: Home and Away
In order to understand properly the specific competitive position of British film-making in both a national and an international market-place, it is necessary to look at some financial performance indicators. One of the most valuable forays into this area is an analysis by Nick Smedley comparing cost and return, at home and in America, of the most successful British films.[11] The first thing he demonstrates is a close correlation between production budget and box-office theatrical receipts: see Table One.

Four immediate points might be taken from this list. Firstly, how few British films were substantial successes in the US. In the period under consideration, only 13 films broke the $10 million barrier. Secondly, although pundits often cite many of these films as the sorts of mainstream cinema the British industry should champion, possibly only *Pink Floyd: The Wall* (1982) really qualifies as a bona fide mainstream film (appealing to the young audience that is the key to success) – the rest are what might be classified as crossover films. They are primarily fairly specialised but with a wider than average audience appeal. Third, it is impossible to pin down the reasons for success and the reasons for this crossover appeal – 'nobody knows anything'. Producers tried to emulate *A Fish Called Wanda* with *The Tall Guy* (1989) with embarrassing results. *Maurice* (1987) and *The Bridge* (1990) both reached nowhere near the success of *A Room with a View* (1985) (although *Howards End*, 1991 and *Enchanted April*, 1991 have rescued the Laura Ashley school for the foreseeable future).[12]

The last, and most significant point, is the relationship between budget (and hence stars, production values, distributor confidence, etc.) and the eventual box-office return (remembering that this anyway is only about one third of the eventual return to an average film). Just as with Hollywood's own movies, the more you spend, the more you get. Unfortunately, unlike Hollywood, British film-makers cannot systematically raise enough money or spend enough to break into the major league where average earnings and occasional stratospheric earnings are sufficient *in toto* to cover the inevitable high miss rate. The basic problem is this: British film-makers, squeezed out of the mainstream global market by the authority of Hollywood, really produce medium-budget films which attempt to cross over from a fairly specialised (discerning adult) market towards a more general appeal. A very few manage this (spectacularly in the case of *A Fish Called Wanda*) but, by and large, it is a strategy that is doomed to fail. Box-office returns are so heavily skewed towards the big-budget, mainstream films, that while an average $20 million movie would come close to covering costs on theatrical release (and make serious money with video and television sales), this is not the case for medium-budget films which on average generate low-to-non-existent US theatrical returns (and consequently small secondary returns). The average cost (at 1991 prices) of the 490 British films produced through the 1980s was approximately £5.78 million.[13] Table One demonstrates that the vast majority of these will earn less than $0.5 million at the US box-office – most of them, indeed, much less. In many cases the costs of distribution will not even be covered and there will certainly be no return to the film-makers. (In passing, it should also be noted that this problem is compounded by the fact that the most successful British films in this list were not funded by British money. For example, *A Fish Called Wanda* was fully financed by MGM).

The reasons for this highly skewed pattern of income are complex. It is partly to do with the 'blockbuster' mentality of studios and audiences, and the distribution and promotional strategies that both reflect and reinforce this mentality. It is also to do with the skewed nature of audience shares. As has been noted, 60 per cent or more of total global audiences is made up of the 12-29 year olds (and half of that total in the US alone). The target audience for the bulk of British movies (the 29 and ups) comprises about 13 per cent of total UK audiences and perhaps only a half per cent of the world total! A runaway success here, even if augmented by a bit of crossover, is still going to be rather modest in the overall scheme of things. And a lesser success will be nowhere.

If the news from America is rather gloomy, is the US market absolutely necessary, Smedley asks, for the survival of a British film industry:

> Given that we find it hard to raise the money to compete in the American market, and given that our success rate is variable and unpredictable, should this particular sacred cow now be slaughtered?[14]

Table Two (also from Smedley) gives some information to think about this question. Unfortunately, however, all the detail is not available for a full comparison with Table One.

This table clearly demonstrates the inadequacy of the UK box-office even to begin to cover costs on more than a very small number of films (during this period almost 200 films were produced in the UK). While these figures do not include income from video and television sales, which in some cases can treble the income, neither do they take into account distributors' and exhibitors' cuts, which takes the lion's share of income. It seems clear that there is no likelihood of systematically raising significant money for re-investment in movies from the UK market. Smedley concludes that, while a few films can turn a profit in the UK market alone,

> the more likely consequence of low to medium budget film-making is really rather inadequate theatrical receipts . . . if a producer decides to up the production values, hire the daughter or son of a famous Hollywood actor, film in exotic locations and imitate the heightened emotions of American cinema, then the American market simply has to be captured.[15]

But as has been demonstrated, the British industry is structurally incapable of systematically and consistently addressing the US market.

A similar picture emerges from another analysis by the BFI which looks at eight features produced in 1990 for which more or less complete statistics are available (see Table Three). While they are not fully representative (at £1.8 million, the average budget is smaller than the UK average overall), they nonetheless indicate some suggestive features. Terry Illot, commenting on these statistics, sardonically identifies the gap between average costs of £1.8 million and average net receipts of £0.8 million as 'the final piece of the jigsaw' that explains the sorry state of the British film industry.[16]

Conclusion and Policy Implications
The preceding discussion paints a gloomy picture of a British film industry, operating in a hostile fiscal environment, squeezed out of the Hollywood-controlled mainstream markets and, therefore, making middle-budget, fairly specialised films which the special-ised markets are too small to sustain. How do we get out of here? And what are the policy implications for film-making in Scotland?

In general there are two sorts of answers to this question. The first is to do with a political and cultural struggle to modify the fiscal disadvantages experienced by the British industry. The second is to do with the types of films produced and the levels of budgets available:

1. The cultural, political and industrial case for state intervention to support a film industry has been widely made. Over the past few years, the most systematic public manifestation of this has been in the post-Downing Street meeting *UK Film Initiatives* monographs published by the BFI.[17] A number of ac-tions are called for:
– fiscal incentives
– a re-structuring of the industry to facilitate re-distribution of rents
– an overseas sales company
– increased support for European co-productions
It is not in the gift of Scottish institutions and organisations to embark upon this strategy unilaterally. Nonetheless, it is essential that the voice of cultural bodies such as the Scottish Film

Production Fund, the Scottish Film Council and the the Scottish
Arts Council are heard strongly in the argument with central
Government. The cultural and economic case has been made – it
now needs to be taken again to government. And, maybe after
that, taken once again . . .

2.   In the absence of a radical shift to a more hospitable operating
climate (and even after then, given the global structure of the
industry), what can film-makers and aspiring film-makers do in
Scotland in order to help themselves? Returning to a broader
picture for a moment, the options facing British film-makers are
summed up by Terry Illot as follows:

> There are two ways of looking at this. Those who are most
> interested in the *capacity* of the production sector in Britain
> would like our investment per film to increase, so that, with
> bigger-budget productions, we will be able to compete with
> Hollywood. Those who look at the *profitability* of British films
> would like budgets to come down. They say that we can't make
> money when our films are so much more expensive than those
> made elsewhere in Europe. [18]

Illot himself favours the former approach, although given the
argument developed above about the more-or-less-impossibility of
genuinely competing with Hollywood this looks like little more
than throwing good money after bad. In a small country like
Scotland, there seems to be no alternative to attempting the
low-budget (say, around £500,000 or below rather than £1.5
million and up) film-making route in order to reduce risk
(particularly to private capital), increase numbers of production
and generate at least the possibility of (modest) profitability across
a slate of production.

What are the financial characteristics of the low-budget film?

i.   Because of the finances of these kinds of films, a much smaller
proportion of any budget would need to be raised from financial
institutions or private sources compared with the medium-budget
film. Potentially, therefore, a substantial proportion could come
from relatively 'soft' sources (i.e. public money – from either
cultural agencies such as the Scottish Film Council and the
Scottish Film Production Fund or from Local Authorities and
Local Enterprise Companies).[19] This shifts the balance of risk and
increases the possibility of securing private and corporate

investment finance. Now, it might be argued that it is not the function of public money to lessen risks to private capital. But surely this is what goes on across Europe. Provided the films emerging from such an arrangement were of genuine cultural value (and this would of course be the key criterion for determining public sector investment), there ought not to be any objection in principle.

ii.   There is reduced reliance on complex pre-sales deals. A film could be financed primarily from local sources and make a sizeable proportion of its costs back from home exhibition and domestic television. Retained rights could then be sold on – probably quite cheaply – but hopefully generating sufficient additional income to enable a production to see a path to break-even if not substantial profit.

iii.   There is a reduced reliance on television money. While TV money will continue to be crucial, it is likely to be harder and harder to find. As Ilott argues:

> The deficit financing of feature films by television companies (by which they invest beyond the value of UK broadcasting rights) may already be a thing of the past. Greater competition among television companies since the advent of cable and satellite, combined with higher exchequer payments by ITV companies, a fall in net advertising revenues in real terms and pressure on costs at the BBC, has already led to considerable rationalisation in the industry. It is likely that, while television will continue to be a major source of funds for feature films, broadcasters will only invest to the extent that can be justified by the UK broadcast rights, forcing film producers to make up the shortfall from other sources while reducing their budgets to a level commensurate with what television can afford.[20]

Taking all this together, in strictly financial terms the future of Scottish film-making could well be *Soft Top, Hard Shoulder* (1992), or *Leon the Pig Farmer* (1992) (which, at costs reported to be around £600,000, including, of course, substantial deferments, stands a good chance of going into profit) rather than *Prague* (1991) (which, at a cost of approximately £2 million, was always unlikely to go into profit). This is not a critical celebration of those films, rather an insistence that their financial structures offer important lessons. Deferments, however, are not one of those lessons. A sustainable film industry cannot make films for £200,000 with, say, a further £400,000 deferred. As a strategy to enable film-makers to spring themselves into the mainstream, it might just work. A cinema that relies on constant self-exploitation and constantly deferred payments is guaranteed to burn out its participants in the shortest possible time.

There are three elements to stimulating a low-low-budget mentality and capacity. The imperative must be, where possible, to minimise financial risk (especially for private capital) and maximise the possibility of profit:

a) Courses, training, seminars, information about low-budget film-making. A commercial low-budget mentality appears to be emerging in the UK. This needs to be nurtured and developed – and where necessary challenged for its lack of cultural daring.

b) A more sophisticated definition of 'profit' and risk. While private investors, bankers and financial institutions obviously will want a stated monetary return on any investment in a film, local authorities and local enterprise companies, for instance, must also take into account the value to their regions of spending by film productions and of supporting production companies and thereby creating jobs. At the same time, the 'return' to a cultural body such as the Scottish Film Production Fund is not just monetary. In other words, different financial inputs into any production could operate on different investment terms and different risk terms (i.e. be in different recoupment positions). The resources available to the Scottish Film Council and the Scottish Film Production Fund would actually enable them to operate as fairly major players in a low-budget film production milieu. It seems plausible that appropriate adjustment to risk terms could facilitate a much needed injection of private capital.

c) A cultural debate. It is not the purpose of this paper to go into this in detail. It is important to note that low-budget film-making is not just a financial but also an aesthetic imperative: films like *Swoon* (1991), *Poison* (1990), *Slacker* (1991), *Edward II* (1991), *Man Bites Dog* (1992) work well not *despite* their budget but *precisely because* they are produced cheaply. If there is one defining characteristic of low-budget film-making it is that it dissolves the distinction between commercial film-making and 'cultural film-making' – it is a meeting ground. But for the Scottish Film Council and the Scottish Film Production Fund to meet and partner private capital in fruitful and mutually beneficial deals, they must articulate a clear and explicit cultural programme – they must be up front about what they want from the deal. A desire for 'good films' is inadequate. Without such a cultural programme, precious arts funding could end up doing little more than propping up (inadequately) commercial film-making. If Scotland is to follow the low-budget route there is an urgent need for a debate about what kinds of stories must be told – what kind of cinema does Scotland need? [21] It is here, not in generating box-office returns, that the Scottish cinemas have a crucial role to play.

There is another significant advantage of going down the low-budget route. It will develop skills and track records so Scottish producers can take advantage of any improvements in the operating environment (if and when this happens), opportunities for co-productions, etc. It is not impossible that in turn this will actually increase the number of *medium-budget* films that occasionally will get made.

At the end of the day, the creation of a Hollywood-style movie industry in Scotland is not viable. We will never see a Hollywood on the Clyde (or, indeed, a Hollywood on the Liffey). A small scale, low-budget industry, using inventive mixes of public and private money, might just be possible. And be sustainable. That, after all, must be one of the key goals of any cultural or any industrial strategy.

Table One

UK FILMS 1980 -1990: COSTS VERSUS US PERFORMANCE

	Cost (£m, 1989 prices)	US box – office ($m, 1989 prices)
Memphis Belle	21.6	26
The Mission	17.6	19.4
The Last Emperor	15.7	46.1
Cry Freedom	15.7	6.4
The Emerald Forest	11.8	28.2
The Killing Fields	10.0	19.0
A Passage to India	9.8	15.8
Gandhi	9.5	32.0
Pink Floyd: The Wall	5.3	11.7
Hope and Glory	4.8	10.9
A Fish Called Wanda	4.5	65.5
Shirley Valentine	4.0	6.1
Buster	3.3	0.5
The Krays	3.2	2.0
Scandal	3.2	8.8
Chariots of Fire	3.0	41.6
Nuns on the Run	3.0	10.1
Educating Rita	2.8	7.1
Local Hero	2.6	3.7
A Room With a View	2.3	23.7
Mona Lisa	2.0	6.5
Wish You Were Here	2.0	3.6
Personal Services	1.65	1.85
My Beautiful Laundrette	0.65	5.6

Source: Smedley (based on *BFI, Variety, Screen International*)

Table Two

UK FILMS 1987 -1990: UK PERFORMANCE VERSUS COST

	UK box-office (£m 1989 prices)	Cost	Balance
A Fish Called Wanda	12.9	4.5	8.4
Shirley Valentine	11.5	4.0	7.5
Wish You Were Here	3.4	2.0	1.4
Buster	4.0	3.3	0.7
Personal Services	2.3	1.65	0.65
Scandal	3.7	3.2	0.5
The Krays	3.3	3.2	0.1
Nuns on the Run	2.9	3.0	-0.1
The Last Emperor	4.4	15.7	-11.3
Cry Freedom	3.7	15.7	-12.0
The Mission	3.0	17.6	-14.6
Memphis Belle	4.4	21.6	-17.2

Source: Smedley (based on *Screen International*, BFI)

Table Three

AVERAGE REVENUES AND COSTS FOR EIGHT UK FILMS

	UK Cinema		UK Video		UK TV		Foreign		Total	
	£	%	£	%	£	%	£	%	£	%
Average Receipts	190,276	17	99,966	9	266,511	23	591,016	51	1,147,768	100
Less costs										
Exhibitor	99,847	9	20,685	2	0	0	0	0	120,531	10.5
Distributor	91,984	8	37,348	3	0	0	7,120	1	136,452	12
Sales Agent	20,919	2	1,691	0	0	0	77,875	7	100,485	9
Balance	*-22,474*	*-2*	*40,242*	*3.5*	*266,511*	*23*	*506,021*	*44*	*790,300*	*68.5*

Note: Eight producers provided a breakdown of their costs and revenues. All the films concerned were made in 1990. Six were primarily TV productions, backed by either the BBC or Channel Four. The budgets for the films ranged between £700,000 and £3.9 million and the average was £1.8million. Average net revenues were £0.8million. Only one film (one which did not mainly involve a broadcaster) went clearly into profit. This film happened to be the one with the second largest budget.

Source: *BFI Film and Television Handbook 1993.*

NOTES

1   London Economics, *The Competitive Position of the European and US Film Industries* (Media Business School, 1993), p. 81.

2   William Goldman, *Adventures in the Screen Trade* (London: Futura, 1985), p.39.

3   For a good overview of this, see Jim Hillier, *The New Hollywood* (London: Studio Vista, 1992), esp. Chapter One.

4   A. Aksoy and K. Robins, 'Hollywood for the 21st Century: Global competition for critical mass in image markets', *Cambridge Journal of Economics*, vol. 16 no. 1, 1992 pp. 1–22.

5   Information on the demographics of global cinema audiences is often confused and contradictory, seeming to have more of the characteristics of urban myth than empirical research. International Media Consultant, James Lee, suggests that, globally, the 15–24 audience might be as much as 80 per cent of the total cinema-going public. See James Lee, presentation to Movie Makars conference, Inverness, 1992, in *Movie Makars: Drama for Film and Television* (Glasgow: Scottish Film Council, 1993). On the other hand, Jim Hillier in *The New Hollywood* suggests that 12–29 year olds make up 56 per cent of cinema audiences in the US. Basing himself on solid CAVIAR research, Andrew Feist indicates that 55 per cent of the total UK audience is made up of 12-24 year olds. See Andrew Feist, 'A Night at the Movies', *Impact*, no. 3, March 1992, pp. 20–22.

6   Michael Porter, *The Competitive Advantage of Nations* (London: Macmillan Press, 1990), pp. 150–1.

7   William Goldman, *Adventures*, p. 80.

8   See *MEDIA: Guide for the Audiovisual Industry* (Brussels: Commission of the European Communities,1992), Edition 8, pp.3–4.

9   Terry Illot, "What Europe really needs", *Impact*, no. 5, August 1992, p.24.

10   London Economics, *The Competitive Position*, pp. 118–9.

11   Nick Smedley, "Didn't We Do Well?", *Impact*, no. 2 , January 1992, pp. 12–14.

12   The Merchant-Ivory films merit some comment. They, and their clones, certainly appear to contradict the argument being developed here that, structurally, there is no home in global film-making for medium-budget films, that there is no middle ground because medium-budget films generally make low returns. It would be foolish to attempt to deny that the Merchant-Ivory English costume drama films have found a medium-budget home. But to celebrate these films, as so many commentators tend to, as the saviours of and the way ahead for the British (English?) film industry begs many questions:

    i   How big is the market for these types of films and can it sustain more than a handful of films a year?

    ii   How robust is the market and can it survive a clutch of poor films or last indefinitely?

    iii   Are there other genres which could supplement it? It is difficult to think of any. In the past, Britain might have enjoyed the Hammer horrors, *Carry On* films, Ealing comedies, and Gainsborough melodramas, but these existed within a very different context – one in which a large proportion of the cost of a film could reliably be earned from home box-office.

    iv   How appropriate is it at the end of the twentieth century for a nation always to 'imagine' itself in the warm glow of Edwardian summers?

v   What would the equivalents look like in Scotland, Wales or Ireland? Answering for the first of these, it would probably look like post-Bill Forsyth whimsy.

These questions are, of course, rhetorical but they do point to the extraordinary difficulty of even contemplating an industry built on such shallow foundations.

13   *BFI Film and Television Handbook 1993* (London: BFI, 1992), p. 20.

14   Smedley, 'Didn't We Do Well?',p.13.

15   ibid.

16   Terry Illot, *BFI Handbook*, p.30.

17   See, particularly, Michael Prescott, *The Need for Tax Incentives* (London: BFI, 1991) and Patricia Perilli, *A Level Playing Field?* (London: BFI, 1991).

18   Illot, *BFI Handbook*, p.30.

19   For more on the two complementary funding bodies for film culture in Scotland, the Scottish Film Council and the Scottish Film Production Fund, see Colin McArthur, "In Praise of a Poor Cinema", *Sight and Sound*, August 1993, pp. 30–32 and elsewhere in this volume; also, Steve McIntyre, "Inventing the Future", *Scottish Film and Visual Arts*, no. 5, Autumn 1993, pp. 17–19.

20   *BFI Handbook*, p.45.

21   The most extensive discussion of this whole issue still remains Colin McArthur (ed.), *Scotch Reels: Scotland in Cinema and Television* (London: BFI, 1982).

THE CULTURAL NECESSITY OF A POOR CELTIC CINEMA

Colin McArthur

There is currently something of a groundswell in favour of 'low-budget/no-budget' film-making in Scotland. Simultaneously, but without prior consultation, several individuals have set in train initiatives which, in diverse ways, have addressed the question. The present writer published a piece in Sight *and Sound* entitled 'In Praise of a Poor Cinema';[1] the former director of the Edinburgh International Film Festival (EIFF), Jim Hickey, announced his move into film production with a series of low-budget 'exploitation' movies based on the practice of Roger Corman in the 1960s in the United States; and the present director of the EIFF, Penny Thomson, included in the 1993 programme two events which broached different aspects of the question: 'Visionary Tactics', which explored the common ground and the contradictions between low-budget orthodox cinema and video art, and a series of viewings and discussions under the heading 'Just Do it'. The latter was mainly concerned with the experience of American independents and particularly with that of Robert Rodriguez whose film *El Mariachi* (1993) was reputedly made for $7,000. The processes of discussion at Edinburgh revealed that even venerable British film institutions like British Screen, up till now mainly associated with orthodox, quasi-European art cinema aesthetics and financial structures, have been attempting to devise mechanisms which would lower budgets drastically.

All of these initiatives *may* represent a challenge to those institutions charged with the public funding of film-making in Scotland, the Scottish Film Council (SFC) and the Scottish Film Production Fund (SFPF), both of which are widely suspected of favouring relatively high-budget, orthodox narrative films which will compete for attention on the European if not the world stage. One says 'suspected' because both bodies operate with a certain degree of sleekitness, to use an evocative Scots word. This is

112

expressed in their claims to be all things to all men while demonstrably making their main financial commitment the attempt to create an orthodox narrative cinema in Scotland. Each body would proclaim its autonomy, but both are chaired by the same man – under the name Allan Schiach, the Chairman of the Macallan Glenlivet whisky firm, and under the name Allan Scott, a successful screenwriter, most notably in his collaborations with Nicolas Roeg. Although the SFPF has assisted diverse types of film (features, documentaries, animations, shorts), its 'Guidelines for Applicants' state that 'the Fund will continue to lean towards the development, and sometimes, to the finance of narrative films'. This policy did not come about as a result of public debate in Scotland. It was the outcome purely of the taste of key figures in the SFC and then of the SFPF, with these institutions increasingly debarring alternatives voices and becoming the preserve of orthodox film industry figures and senior television executives. The final element accelerating the gadarene rush to film as commodity in Scotland was the setting up in 1993 of the Glasgow Film Fund. Doubtless created through the active lobbying of the SFC and the SFPF, it currently stands at £155,000 per annum made up of contributions from the Glasgow Development Agency, Strathclyde Business Development, Glasgow City Council and the European Regional Development Fund. Unsurprisingly, it will be administered by the SFPF and its criteria are frankly commercial. Only feature films with a budget of £500,000 or over may apply and its main function is to increase spending, through film production, in the local economy. The SFPF has committed the entire first year allocation of funds to only one project and Glasgow City Council is already turning down applications from low-budget film-makers they formerly might have supported on the basis that all their film funding is now going to be channelled through the Glasgow Film Fund. And all of this has happened within an economic discourse which has explicitly excluded the consideration of issues of representation and cultural identity, issues markedly to the forefront of many low-budget film-makers' concerns.

It might be thought that the SFC, an ostensibly cultural body, would have held itself at arm's length from some of these developments, but it has been an enthusiastic cheerleader to them all. It recently produced the *Charter for the Moving Image in Scotland*, an attempt to indicate what ought to be done on the various

Scottish film fronts and the institutions needed to do it. Several responses, not least that of the producers association, PACT (Scotland), have criticised its 'productivist' discourse, its advocacy of production – any kind of production – at any price. It is mentioned here to indicate the extent to which its proposals (e.g. the uniting of all publicly-funded film mechanisms into one Scottish Screen Agency) are hand in glove with the centralising, giganticising, market-driven production ideology of the SFPF.

It was the SFC too which, along with the SFPF, co-mounted Movie Makars (sic), an event designed to bring the forms of classical Hollywood screenwriting to Scotland. Its lavish report, which cost £3,600 to produce, indicates the style and ethos of the event and the world-view which permeates it. Its title page carries a photograph of Allan Scott and William Goldman, the 'star' of the proceedings. The event's genesis can be gathered from the quasi-theological dedication in the report to 'Allan Scott (the inspiration) who in manifest and incalculable ways provides the spirit of Movie Makars'. The bringing of Allan Schiach/Scott – with his dual discourse of business and Hollywood – into the Scottish film cultural picture would make an interesting case study. My own reading is that his arrival, probably the result of lobbying of the Scottish Office by the SFC and the SFPF, further demonstrates their capacity to misjudge what Scottish cinema actually needs, both economically and culturally.

Movie Makars can be read as an instance of British film culture's growing obsession with 'story structure'. An intrinsically interesting discourse which renders explicit the Hollywood writing practices of half a century, 'story structure' entered Britain by way of screenwriting handbooks such as those by Syd Field and, most dramatically, through Robert McKee's much hyped story-structure courses. The discourse's value is to spell out the elements of the classic Hollywood two-hour script; how stories are articulated, developed and resolved; how characters are given motivation; at what point stories need to be 'turned' and so on. Its down side is that it tends to fetishise this specific form of storytelling, to render it 'natural' and other ways aberrant. With one stroke it wipes off the agenda alternative ways of thinking and making cinema. By the criteria of the 'story-structure' discourse, film-makers such as Eisenstein, Rossellini, Ozu, Bresson, Godard, Makavejev, Jarman and countless others would be deemed failures. Needless to add, Movie Makars is wholly complicit with

the production ideology of the SFC and the SFPF and many of
its participants (by invitation only) were either members or
beneficiaries of the Fund.

What then has this increasingly market-driven policy delivered
to Scottish film culture? In its decade or so of existence, the SFPF
has assisted about fifty projects, about one fifth of which (though
an increasing trend) have been feature films, the remainder being
shorts, documentaries and animation projects. Though one might
wish to commend the competence (and occasionally the
excellence) of particular films, one would be hard-pressed to
describe the sense in which they constitute a Scottish film
movement, a historically specific grappling with the contradictions
of the Scottish past and present, a set of recurrent themes and
styles discernibly amounting to a *collectivity.* What we have, rather,
is a rag-bag of films which, competitively and individualistically,
have clawed their way through the available Scottish, UK or
pan-European funding mechanisms. There are startlingly few
titles in the list which have achieved any kind of critical reputation,
perhaps only *Tree of Liberty* (1987), *Venus Peter* (1989), *Play Me
Something* (1989), *Silent Scream* (1989) and *Tickets for the Zoo* (1991).
Part of the problem is, of course, that there has been no systematic
attempt to generate critical writing about them or to address the
extent to which they might relate to each other (of which more
below).

The most serious misgivings about the policy have been
expressed over *Prague* (1990). Out of an annual subvention of (at
the time) about £250,000 per annum, the SFPF put £130,000 into
Prague over two years. It seems to have been a commercial failure
with no British distributor picking it up but, even more seriously,
questions are being asked about its relevance to Scottish history
and culture. Virtually its only claim to be connected with Scotland
(having been shot in Prague largely with French money) is that
some of its personnel – producer Christopher Young, producer/
director Ian Sellar and actor Alan Cumming – are Scots. With its
budget of £2million made up from diverse countries and funding
mechanisms, *Prague* has about it the petrified feel of a
Euro-pudding, connecting with no actually existing society except
perhaps that of the European art house. The case of *Prague* does
not encourage a 'thumbs up' for either the SFPF's (unspoken)
cultural policies or its economic ones, but the latter might be
better judged over the next two years when some of its projects in

development hit the screen. These are marked by some well-known names such as writer Alan Sharp and directors Ken Loach, David Hayman and Michael Caton-Jones. These projects intensify the tendency for funding to be sought from diverse mechanisms: British Screen, the Glasgow Film Fund, and SCRIPT, the European Script Development Fund, loom large in the data so far released about them.

The current pervasiveness of 'market-speak' in Scottish film affairs these days has two noticeable effects. Firstly, it inflates budgets. This is true not only at the high end of the scale, like *Prague*, but, even more perniciously, at the bottom end as well. Two events, occurring simultaneously, illustrate this. The SFPF issued a press release announcing that, in association with BBC Scotland, it had invested £90,000 in three short films: £30,000 per ten-minute short. In accordance with the SFPF's overall ideology of production, they were to be 'narrative shorts' and it is envisaged that their makers will 'springboard from the making of a short on to a first feature film'. The project was called 'Tartan Shorts', a singularly offensive title which reveals a massive ignorance, among those involved, of the regressive character of Tartanry in Scottish culture. (Its defenders would contend that the title represents an ironic, postmodernist playing with that tradition). Concurrently with the issue of the press release, the SFPF sent out a letter to two young, Scots-based film/video makers, Douglas Aubrey and Alan Robertson, turning down their request for £15,000 to complete their *feature-length* road movie, *Work, Rest and Play* (1992). By a sharp irony, one of the recipients of the £30,000 grants was the actor Peter Capaldi, writer of the amusing but empty road movie, *Soft Top, Hard Shoulder* (1992), which has none of the 'condition of Britain' quality of *Work, Rest And Play*. Once again, the SFPF demonstrated graphically its commitment to orthodox financial structures and orthodox aesthetics – *Work, Rest, And Play*, for example, makes extensive use of electronic imaging and computerised procedures.

The second effect of the pervasiveness of 'market-speak' in Scottish film affairs is that it has created a climate within which to utter the word 'culture' is to elicit pitying smiles. While the official documents of the SFC and the SFPF make ritual obeisances to 'Scottish film culture', no indications are forthcoming as to the content of that culture. Reliant upon the single ineffable concept of 'talent' to decide the validity of a project, the SFC and the SFPF do not (as institutions, although certain of their officers as individuals do) have the analytic resources or categories to explain what the concept of a 'Scottish film culture' might mean or how it might relate to wider Scottish cultural or social questions. The individual projects they invest in, awarded on the 'talent' of the grantees, cannot be read by these institutions as other than separate, autonomous films having no connection with each other or with Scottish history and contemporary culture.

The absence of a cultural discourse from the SFC or the SFPF can be indicated by their failure even to perceive the problem which was thrown up recently in the research findings of a Scottish development agency. The research, among top German industrialists, revealed that the image of Scotland inside their heads led them to conclude that Scotland was a good country to rest in but not invest in. Scottish cultural studies academics knew immediately the historical reasons for this: Scotland's coming to the forefront of the European imagination, principally through the phenomena of Ossianism and Sir Walter Scott, in the period after 1770; the consequent construction of images of Scotland and the Scots taking place outside of Scotland and having more to do with the aims, needs, fears and fantasies of the emergent European bourgeoisie than with the self-image of the Scots; and the complex of historical factors (not least the de-politicisation of nationalism in Scotland) which caused the Scots increasingly to live within images of themselves enunciated elsewhere. Although the historical experience of the Scots is quite specific and cannot be conflated with that of other peoples, their representation in discourse has something in common with that of other 'subordinate' groups. The word 'subordinate' with regard to the Scots must be put in inverted commas since it is part of their specificity that they were/are not subordinate – or not pertinently so – in economic terms. As Tom Nairn has pointed out, Scotland was a well-rewarded junior partner in the imperial enterprise.[2] The subordination of the Scots has been on the terrain of discourse.

It is useful to think of the process of the discursive construction of the Celt as a by-product of the European bourgeoisie's construction of its own identity. As is so often the case, that identity was formulated by creating a monstrous Other who bore all the 'negative' features the European bourgeois (*homo oeconomicus*) did not wish to have. The process can be represented as a series of binary oppositions thus:

homo oeconomicus	*homo celticus*
urban	rural
civilised	uncivilised
barbered	hirsute
ambitious	shiftless
cultured	natural
'masculine'	'feminine'

The oppositions are potentially endless. The point of articulation, the controlling point of utterance and definition of identity is always *homo oeconomicus* and never *homo celticus*. The process, in its historical and geographical diversity (*homo pacificus, homo africanus,* 'woman') has been explored by Franz Fanon, Edward Said, Homi Bhabha and others.[3]

As well as understanding the problem thrown up by the German industrialists, Scots cultural studies academics know what needs to be done – the confronting and deconstruction of the regressive, disempowering discourses within which the Celt has been constructed and their replacement with discourses more appropriate to a modern, industrial, multi-racial Scotland. This is a position arrived at intuitively by certain Scottish film-makers, e.g. Brian Crumlish in *The Caledonian Account* (1976) and Murray Grigor in *Scotch Myths* (1982), but it is an understanding that has not penetrated to the SFC or the SFPF. Hooked on the notion of 'talent', they see no need for cultural discourse, no need for a film-making strategy which might help dislodge regressive ideas about Scotland from the heads of German industrialists, among others.

Clearly, the framework of ideas within which the Celt was constructed, initially over the period 1770 to 1830, became disseminated over every available sign-system: literature, painting, opera, ballet, fashion, post-cards and – with increasing momentum in the twentieth century – advertising, cinema and television. The collection of essays, *Scotch Reels: Scotland in Cinema and Television,* is substantially about this historical process, in particular how the cinemas of Hollywood and Ealing have constructed the Scots, the apotheoses of these traditions being *Brigadoon* (1954) and *The Maggie* (1953) respectively.[4] Clearly an analogous process was at work with regard to the discursive construction of Ireland. *The Maggie* and *The Quiet Man* (1953) are discursively almost identical – an American being humanised and 'feminised' through his encounter with the 'other-worldly' Celtic milieu. Needless to say, this historical process whereby particular groups are constructed as having no 'head' but only 'heart', no capacity for politics or economics, only 'feeling', is the ideological equivalent of the material expropriations of colonialism and imperialism. Indeed, Malcolm Chapman, in his magisterial study *The Gaelic Vision in Scottish Culture* calls the process 'symbolic appropriation'.[5] The truly terrifying dimension of this, however, is that *homo celticus* will come to live within the discursive categories fashioned by the oppressor to the extent of casting himself in the imposed role in the stories he makes about himself. Franz Fanon explores this in relation to blacks in *Black Skin, White Masks*. The *locus tragicus* of this with regard to Scotland is, of course, *Local Hero* (1983). As in *The Maggie*, a hard-nosed American executive comes to Scotland to set up an oil terminal but, softened through his encounter with 'dream Scotland', opts instead for an observatory and marine life sanctuary. The Scottish women he meets are called Stella and Marina, the sky and the sea: Scotland is 'Nature'. What distinguishes *Local Hero* from *Brigadoon* and *The Maggie* is that its director, Bill Forsyth, has spent his entire life in Scotland. The chilling fact is that, in its representation of Scotland, *Local Hero* is ideologically indistinguishable from the earlier films.

It is at this point that economics and culture intersect and where the argument for the *cultural* necessity of a *poor Celtic cinema* becomes most compelling. *Local Hero* was the first film of Bill Forsyth aimed at the international market. It was produced and 'packaged' by David Puttnam precisely in those terms. So internationally ramified has the *homo celticus* discourse become in the two centuries or so since its articulation that movies about Scotland or Ireland which are not formulated within it, or exist in some relationship with it, are likely to be quite literally 'unreadable' to a wide, international audience. To go back once more to the German executives: they know that Scotland is about rest and recuperation, about escape from the harsh worlds of politics and economics, about letting the wells fill up through exposure to a people in touch with the 'eternal verities'. To present them with different kinds of stories would seriously disorient them. It is not by accident that *Local Hero* is a cult film in Germany and elsewhere. To offer an axiom to Celtic film-makers: the more your films are consciously aimed at an international market, the more their conditions of intelligibility will be bound up with regressive discourses about your own culture.

The 'market-speak' of the SFC and the SFPF – and possibly of analogous institutions in other Celtic countries – is thus a recipe for the continuing discursive entrapment of the Celtic peoples. The lack of recognition by the SFC and the SFPF of any discursive problem is paralleled by the lack of awareness among individual film-makers that they are living within regressive discourses. This is a problem which goes beyond film-making to suffuse the whole of Scottish culture, so much so that the present writer has felt it necessary to fashion the concept of 'the Scottish discursive unconscious' to try to explain the phenomenon.[6] What seems to happen is that when Scots are required to deal with particular aspects of their own history, certain narrative forms and tones come into play unconsciously, on 'automatic pilot', so to speak. It happens over a range of Scottish 'moments' but is particularly marked with respect to the Gaelteachd. The process was writ large at the tercentenary of the Massacre of Glencoe in January 1992 during which most of the Scottish press adopted an elegiac (often emotionally self-lacerative) tone oscillating around images of solitude and loss. Press photographs were often of gnarled, leafless trees on desolate hillsides and one writer spoke of the rain mingling with the tears of the onlookers as they recalled the shameful events of 1692. One shudders to imagine the emotional self-indulgence which is bound to accompany the two hundred and fiftieth anniversary of the Jacobite Rebellion of 1745-6 in 1995, an anniversary which will incorporate that cynosure for the glorification of sorrow – the Battle of Culloden. One cannot but agree with Malcolm Chapman's view that, despite the suffering which it entailed, many Scots intellectuals are glad Culloden occurred. A more charitable view of the flagellation Scots visit on themselves in their art and discourse when dealing with Glencoe, Culloden, the Highland Clearances or, in a more contemporary example, the demise of shipbuilding on the Upper Clyde, is that they are indeed not wholly responsible for their actions, that they are largely under the sway of 'the Scottish discursive unconscious'. If their country and its history have been constructed, by voices outside Scotland, within a discourse which places *homo celticus* in a timeless, unchanging dream-world existing to transform the stranger, what other response is possible when contemplating the reality of Scottish history and contemporary life than to mourn the land of lost content.

It is one of the delusions of the SFC and the SFPF that this inheritance has no purchase on the sensibilities of contemporary Scots film-makers, can be sloughed off in the grand march to 'Hollywood on the Clyde'. It is a dismal paradox that the more grandiose their delusions become, the higher they rack up film budgets, the more firmly they proclaim film as commodity, the more surely will they become mired in regressive discourses about their country. If they only knew it, their only salvation lies in a *poor Celtic cinema*. The term *poor cinema* was suggested by the title of the 1950s Italian art movement *arte povera* within which art-works were made out of the materials which were to hand and which would consequently not need to compete with the glitzy and financially inflated world of the gallery circuit. However, its cinematic lineage goes back rather longer, certainly being discernible in the quasi-artisanal practice of the British documentary movement of the 1930s, in post-war Italian neo-realism, in the French *nouvelle vague* and, not least, in certain Third World cinematic practices in which distinctions among film-makers, critics and audiences might be eroded.[7] In all of these instances, however, the films were low-budget not just for economic reasons, but in order to be able to say things which remained unsaid in more orthodox structures and practices.

What then would a *poor Celtic cinema* look like in both economic and cultural terms? The *BFI Film And Television Handbook* of 1993 profiled eight recent British feature films. The most important information thrown up was that, while the average budget was £1.8m, the average box-office return was £0.8m.[8] Basic micawberish economics would suggest that, at the very least, no budget within a *poor Celtic cinema* should exceed £0.8m, but eminently economically well-founded film production practices, such as that of James Mackay (whose productions and budgets have included *What Can I Do With A Male Nude?* 1985, £5,000, *Man To Man* 1991, £155,000, and *The Last Of England* 1987, £250,000) suggest that the absolute upper limit should be £300,000. Even this figure is large in relation to the public monies available for film-making in Scotland. Excluding the £10 million or so allocated by the Gaelic Television Committee, which has a special linguistic aim and may not in the long term be renewable, there is currently about £0.5 million spread over three or four mechanisms. Budgets

considerably smaller than existing ones, predicated upon
different aesthetic strategies, would be possible, but, as the case of
Work, Rest And Play indicates, this is not a road the SFPF intends to
go down. A demand that budgets should not exceed £300,000
(and this envisages inputs from other non-Scottish mechanisms)
should be the centrepiece of the call for a *poor Celtic cinema.* A key
consideration in awarding grants should be the degree of
imagination (potentially) displayed by the awardee working with
limited resources. This would compare well with the present
long-winded system of 'development' monies, innumerable drafts
of scripts and bloated sums being paid to a few elite personnel.

As well as drastically curtailing the size of budgets, the SFC and
the SFPF must develop low cost production facilities which will
enable awardees to realise their projects without recourse to costly
hire facilities. Clearly the best way to achieve this is to strengthen
the already existing Scottish film and video workshops so that they
become 'enabling houses'. The Scottish workshops never attained
the status and level of funding of their southern analogues. There
were complex reasons for this, not least the presence in England
and Wales of substantial cadres of independents who, through
active organisations like the Independent Film-Makers
Association, got into a devastatingly effective relationship with the
(then) ACTT, the major film and television technicians union.
This relationship wielded extraordinary leverage on the BFI,
strengthening the hand of sympathetic figures within that
organisation to produce the *Workshop Declaration* and the series of
BFI/Channel Four funded workshops. In retrospect, they proved
to be problematic creations, not least for the sense of
exclusiveness generated among those fortunate to have acquired
long-term production funding through attachment to one of the
recognised workshops. Eventually they fell apart as funding levels
and ideologies changed within the BFI and Channel Four. One of
the main reasons the Scots equivalents did not advance so
markedly was the indifference bordering on contempt for
workshops historically displayed by the SFC and the SFPF.

The First Reels project illustrates the lack of thought given by
the major Scots institutions to the workshops. Jointly funded by
the SFC and Scottish Television, First Reels gave grants of between
£100 and £2,000 in its first year to thirty applicants. The project
gave no thought to how the awardees might produce their
material. Predictably, they turned for help to the already

resource-starved Scottish workshops and small, independent production companies which, giving what help they could, made their irritation plain to the SFC. It is to be hoped that the SFC, and the SFPF, will recognise that proper funding of the Scottish workshops is the way to ensure that a Scottish film-making culture evolves, and not the springboarding of a few individuals into international film production. At the same time, these organisations should learn from the experience of England and Wales that workshops should be enabling houses rather than production houses.

In opposition to the marked literary bias of the present system in which a disproportionate weight is given to scripts, awardees within a *poor Celtic cinema* should be required to demonstrate their *cinematic* literacy in the sense of understanding the aesthetic traditions they propose working in. This will be read perversely as a requirement that awardees have an A-Level in Film Studies. Nothing of the kind! However, it might be expected of awardees that they would know what a film looked like if made by Sergei Eisenstein, Fritz Lang, John Ford, Roberto Rossellini, Yasujiro Ozu, Vincente Minnelli, Kenneth Anger, Jean-Luc Godard or Michael Snow. My impression is that the vast majority of applicants to and beneficiaries of the various grant-giving mechanisms are not ciné-literate, or not systematically so in a way that would help produce a *poor Celtic cinema*. The harsh economic climate of the last decade has all but eradicated the policy of retrospectives in publicly-subsidised film theatres and film festivals in the UK, and video availability has not wholly compensated for this. A generation of film-makers is emerging which will have been exposed almost exclusively to classic and contemporary Hollywood movies and selected European art cinema. It is quite likely that only a minority of them will have seen a movie by Pudovkin or Vertov, Norman McLaren or Len Lye, Mizoguchi or Oshima, Vigo or Bresson, Wajda or Has, Lindsay Anderson or Bill Douglas, and so on. It would doubtless be regarded as quaint by the SFC and the SFPF if it were suggested to them that they might systematically programme, document and debate those elements in the history of cinema which demonstrate the most imaginative deployment of limited resources. One has in mind films like Jean-Luc Godard's *Les Carabiniers* (1963), Dusan Makavejev's *The Switchboard Operator* (1967) and Peter Bogdanovich's *Targets* (1967) which 'cannibalise' previously existing footage. The SFC runs the

Scottish Central Film Library which contains, among other things, the entire output of Films of Scotland, the sponsored documentary mechanism which was the seedbed for the older generation of Scots film-makers. Many of these films cry out for critical deconstruction, not least on account of the representations they offer of Scotland and the Scots. Equally imaginatively austere are those innumerable films in the cinema's history which are wholly or partly made up of still images. Chris Marker's *La Jetée* (1963) and Alain Resnais' *Nuit Et Brouillard* (1955) spring to mind. Some of the early films of Hans-Jürgen Syberberg – most notably *Ludwig, Requiem For A Virgin King* (1972) – delivered an incredible richness of image by using not built sets but blown-up transparencies. On the sound front, a considerable number of the cinema's most distinguished films have used wild tracks, in whole or part, often in the voice-over mode. Bresson and Godard come to mind here.

The concept of *poor cinema* has already provoked howls of derision, being travestied – usually by those with a vested interest in preserving more orthodox film-making practices – as 'films nobody wants to see'. The implication is that *poor cinema* must of necessity consist of avant-garde, difficult, perhaps (to use one of the terms of the 1970s debates) 'unpleasurable' works. On the contrary, *poor cinema* should not be prescriptive about aesthetic forms (the besetting sin of the 'anti-Hollywood/Mosfilm' position in the 1970s debates) and should certainly accomodate quite traditional narrative movies such as Peter Bogdanovich's *Targets* and Robert Rodriguez's *El Mariachi*. However, it should be noted simply as a historical fact that the makers of low-budget, traditional narrative movies often see them as stepping-stones to careers in the orthodox industry, as is evidenced by the alacrity with which Hollywood snapped up both Bogdanovich and Rodriguez.

A condition of award within a *poor Celtic cinema* should be that the proposed film deal in some sense with the *contradictions* of the Celtic past and present. That is, it should display a sense of history and society, should be manifestly rooted in the society from which it comes. *Prague* is only the most recent and notorious example of the practice of funding films which could be taking place on another planet for all the relevance they bear to their countries of origin. The cardinal error of bodies like the SFC and the SFPF is to assume that a 'Scottish cinema' will come into being by making a series of one-off films and 'marketing' them as such through festivals.There is nothing more pitiable than the sight of gaggles of film bureaucrats (regrettably, Scots now among them) hovering around the fringes of festivals such as Cannes in vain attempts to 'market' their films. Recalling how 'rag-bag' the decade's production by the SFPF looks, the lesson has to be learned that national cinemas or film movements do not simply happen, they are in great measure *constructed*. Movements such as (to take only post-war examples) Italian neo-realism, Polish cinema of the 1950s, the French new wave, Czech Cinema of the 1960s, and Brazilian *cinema novo* were perceived as such mainly because they were constructed in film criticism and journalism as constituting collectivities, diverse within and among themselves to be sure, but collectivities nevertheless, specific cinematic responses to complex national moments. International critical recognition helped finance the continuing existence of these movements. If the cultural questions are properly addressed, the economic questions will take care of themselves. It is the bitter experience of (some?) of the Celtic countries that this formulation has been reversed. I await with bated breath the first critical articles, special magazine issues, cinémathèque seasons and festival retrospectives which will proclaim the arrival of *le nouveau cinéma pauvre celtique*!

NOTES

1 Colin McArthur, 'In Praise of a Poor Cinema', S*ight and Sound*, August 1993, pp. 30–32.
2 Tom Nairn, *The Break-Up of Britain* (London:Verso, 1981).
3 Franz Fanon, *Black Skin,White Masks* (London: Pluto, 1986 edition); Edward Said,*Orientalism* (London: RKP, 1978); Homi Bhabha (ed.), *Nation and Narration* (London: Routledge, 1990).
4 Colin McArthur (ed.), *Scotch Reels: Scotland in Cinema and Television* (London:British Film Institute,1982).
5 Malcolm Chapman,*The Gaelic Vision in Scottish Culture* (London: Croom Helm,1978), p.28.
6 Colin McArthur, 'Scottish Culture: a Reply to David McCrone', *Scottish Affairs*, no.4, Summer 1993.
7 Jim Pines and Paul Willemen (eds.), *Questions of Third Cinema* (London: British Film Institute,1989).
8 'UK Film, Television and Video: Statistical Overview', *BFI Film and Television Yearbook 1993* (London: BFI,1992), p.30.

CULTURE, INDUSTRY AND IRISH CINEMA

Kevin Rockett

Introduction

Is it culture, or is it an industry? This decades-old debate about film has had an unbalanced history in Ireland. Until the 1980s, Irish state policy for fiction film production largely ignored the cultural value of film in favour of an industrial policy which sought to develop film as no more than a branch of manufacturing. The long, hard fight over many decades by Irish film activists to raise national consciousness in favour of an indigenous Irish cinema only began to achieve significant results in the 1980s. The debate between those favouring a cultural cinema, and those asserting an industrial model for Irish film production, is still far from ended. Indeed, some 'progressive' film voices would still take the view that it is an Irish film 'industry' rather than an Irish cinema which the revived Bord Scannán na hÉireann/Irish Film Board (BSE) is responsible for establishing. Perhaps the only way in which this dichotomy is ever likely to be resolved is through an acceptance of both the economic and cultural merits of film production.

However the long ascendancy of the industrial model for film production has certainly inhibited the development of an Irish cinema. It has also skewed debates about film, as when the first Bord Scannán was wound down in 1987. At that time, and in response to the so-called divisions within the film 'community', a form of 'broad-frontism' evolved in which some film activists sought to answer the distorted economic/industrial arguments of the state, and so-called 'commercial' film-makers, in their own terms, rather than shifting the terms of the debate decisively into the cultural arena.

Given the revitalised film environment which followed the initiatives of 1993, it is important that this legacy is not forgotten. For example, much praise has been directed at the high technical standards and production values in the short films emanating in

126

recent years from Dun Laoghaire College of Art and Design and the Department of Communications, Rathmines, as well as from Film Base and many younger independent film-makers. The 'look' of these films, compared with the films of the older and more established generation of film-makers working in the same gauge (16mm) a decade ago, is far superior. But, when a wide selection of these films is viewed together, it is hard not to come to the conclusion that many of them lack the critical or cultural engagement so evident in the films of their predecessors. Or, to put it another way, perhaps the pull of the 'industry' is such that many of these films are so neutral, almost 'content-free', that they lack any persuasive critical, cultural or political engagement with Irish society at all. While criticisms were directed at the first generation of independent fiction film-makers at the level of form or production values, their films were generally regarded as committed critical engagements with Irish culture and society. This comparison may appear unfair to young film-makers who have perhaps only made one, or at most two, short films and who would argue that there are new aesthetic parameters now guiding contemporary film practice. Be that as it may, the post-1987 film environment has, nonetheless, witnessed the restoration of the ascendancy of the industrial model for film production over a culturally engaged, critical cinema in Ireland.

At the other end of the film production scale, the pull of the international commercial film industry for other Irish film-makers has often been such as to re-cycle, even revitalise, the stereotypes of British and American cinema versions of Ireland. Notwithstanding the greater complexity and maturity of film in Ireland at all levels, the point of departure for any discussion of film policy must be to re-examine the decisive role the state has played historically, often through neglect rather than active initiatives, in fostering an Irish cinema, and reinforcing narrow notions of cultural protectionism and industrial development.

Ireland in the International Context

Ireland occupies a position within the global film economy which is all too familiar to countries and regions which have small populations and which are dependent on metropolitan capitalist economies. Ireland's share of global box-office, at less than 0.5 per cent, illustrates this relative weakness. Ireland's peripherality as regards the cinema remains defined in relation to Britain and the

USA. Bound to these societies since the mid-nineteenth century by a common language, Ireland was easily penetrated by both silent and sound cinemas. A process of Irish cultural resistance, after independence in 1922, to foreign popular culture, most especially the cinema, was fuelled by a mixture of quixotic, nativist cultural policies and a conservative Christian morality which sought to exclude from Ireland, through statutory means, any image or word which might infringe the pre-modernist ideology of the Irish Catholic Church. The result was a film censorship regime which used the subjective terms 'indecency, obscenity and blasphemy', as well as the all-encompassing phrase 'contrary to public morality', to ban about 3,000 films, and cut another 8,000, during the first four decades of independence. Many other films were never submitted to the Official Censor during those decades as they too would have suffered a similar fate. While this protectionist policy led to restrictions on the availability of British and American cinema in Ireland, it did not encourage the state to support alternative cinematic images of Ireland which might have challenged the perceived shortcomings of foreign cinema.

Production
Since the 1930s, the state's support for film production has usually been limited to addressing problems of unemployment through encouraging foreign capital to invest in films in Ireland. As a result, there was little in the way of productive dialogue between the artisanal or small-scale indigenous film-makers and the large-scale foreign film producers who were being encouraged by the state to make films in Ireland. In pursuit of this policy, the state supported the establishment of Ireland's only film studios at Ardmore in 1958. The studios' legacy of indebtedness and bankruptcy, under both private and state ownership, encouraged a shift from support for fixed plant to direct aid for Irish film production by the 1980s. But, insofar as a state policy for film existed, it continued to emphasise, even in the 1980s, the development of a market-oriented, non-subsidised indigenous industry. It was, though, a state body, Bord Scannán, operating with limited financial resources of only about IR£0.5 million per annum during 1981–87, which made the most significant contribution to the development of an Irish cinema.

During its six years existence Bord Scannán was allocated IR£3.06 million as capital for investment in films. This was a revolving fund whereby the money invested in projects would be re-invested in future productions. BSE part-funded ten feature films, twenty short fiction films and documentaries for television, as well as fifteen experimental shorts. It also provided development loans and grants to approximately sixty projects to assist in script development and pre-production work. Although supporting a broad range of commercial and cultural films, BSE had, by the end of its tenure in 1987, increasingly moved towards 'commercial' film interests.

The Board advanced IR£1.247 million to the ten feature projects, of which only IR£0.106 million, or 8.5 per cent, had been repaid by February 1992. While this poor financial return was presented as a reason for closing Bord Scannán, this narrow approach ignored the quite considerable additional sums which these ten projects generated, including Irish investments of IR£1.615 million and foreign investment of IR£3.295, out of total budgets of IR£6.157 million for the ten films. Only two of the projects, with total budgets of IR£0.708 million, were fully funded from Irish sources. Even in national economic terms, these figures demonstate the key role played by BSE in that its 20 per cent stake opened up the possibility of other Irish and foreign film investment in films made by Irish film-makers. With the demise of Bord Scannán the level of activity in low to medium-budget feature films declined significantly, though the production of very low-budget shorts grew exponentially.

As part of the new 'commercial' regime, corporate and individual tax concessions for investment in film production were introduced. The most important scheme, Section 35 of the 1987 Finance Act, allowed for up to IR£600,000 to be invested by a qualifying company over three years, and the investment could be deducted from a company's total profits. However, the sum invested could not exceed 60 per cent of a qualifying film's total budget, and at least 75 per cent of the production work had to be carried out in Ireland. This led during the period from 1987 to 1992 to a total of $9.4 million being invested in eleven projects. This scheme was subsequently extended to 1995. Another tax-based scheme, the Business Expansion Scheme, allowed for an individual investor to obtain tax relief of up to IR£75,000 for new investment in a qualifying film company, though only IR£25,000 could be invested in any one year. During 1987–91 this scheme allowed ten projects to raise $1.18 million. Despite the fact that the state was writing off revenue, these tax write-offs to corporate and commercial film investors were not generally regarded as a form of state subsidy and inevitably this distorted the film production debate after 1987.

The formation of the historic coalition government of Fianna Fáil and Labour at the end of 1992 decisively altered the film environment in Ireland. It is not in the nature of Irish politics to make dramatic changes in policy. Yet, the six months from September 1992 to March 1993 was not just a period of turbulent political development, but was also arguably the most concentrated period of change ever for Irish film culture. With the opening of the Irish Film Centre in September 1992 by An Taoiseach (Prime Minister), Albert Reynolds, a new confidence not only permeated the whole Irish film community, now that at last it had a 'home', but An Taoiseach announced the establishment of a Working Group on the Film Industry with a brief to report within three months. However, the Fianna Fáil/ Progressive Democrats coalition government of that time collapsed before the report was completed. With protracted negotiations for a new government taking place, it seemed that another opportunity for film was fading fast. As a result, the phoenix that arose was both unexpected and exhilarating. Not only was Ireland to have its first Minister for Arts, Culture and the Gaeltacht with full Cabinet rank, but, in the person of Labour's Michael D. Higgins, the post was also to have a radical and informed voice on culture.

In the previous year four reports on film production in Ireland had been produced: besides the Working Party Report, Film-Makers Ireland, Film Base, and Irish Film Centre/ Temple Bar Properties had all produced well-researched contributions to the debate. At last, the bullet was bitten. On the morning of Neil Jordan's and Michelle Burke's Oscar wins (witnessed by the Minister and his arts adviser at an all-night Oscar party at the Film Centre), the Cabinet decided to re-activate Bord Scannán. An allocation of IR£1.1 million in 1993 will increase to an annual budget of about IR£2.5 million from 1994, with a review of the Board's performance after three years. When the Minister announced a week later that film activist Lelia Doolan was being appointed Chairperson of the Board, there was further cause for rejoicing, as her record of working at all levels of film, television and theatre had demonstrated a commitment to indigenous culture in an international context.

Further pieces to make up the total film and television cultural jigsaw were also put in place by the new Minister. The 'cap' on Radio Telefis Éireann's (RTE's) advertising revenue, the main excuse given by RTE for the reduction in programmes being commissioned from independent film-makers, was lifted. In addition, Higgins set out a clear requirement that RTE increase its commissions from independents. RTE's 1993 commissions of IR£3.5 million are due to increase to IR£5 million in 1994, rising to IR£12.5 million by 1999. To help achieve this objective, RTE has appointed a commissioning editor for independent productions. The long-campaigned-for Telifis na Gaeilge was initiated with a Coiste Bunaithe (Founding Committee), chaired by Gearoid 0 Tuathaigh, the Vice-President of University College Galway. Capital and other start-up costs for the service are estimated at about IR£15 million, while an annual subvention of about IR£15 million will be required to provide three hours of Irish language programmes per day. It is intended that RTE will provide one hour of these, while the other two hours will be commissioned from the independent sector.

Important tax changes were also introduced. In the 1993 Finance Act additional concessions were made to those investing in film via Section 35 and Business Expansion Scheme-type finance. These changes include increasing the sums which can be invested in a film project under Section 35 from IR£200,000 to IR£350,000 per annum, and from IR£600,000 to IR£1,050,000 over three years. A separate and additional Business Expansion Scheme was established whereby an individual can invest IR£25,000 per annum for three years in a film project in addition to the IR£25,000 which can be invested in non-film Business Expansion Schemes. Section 35, unlike its earlier versions, can now be used in co-productions, with only the requirement that the percentage of the project which has been invested from Ireland be spent in Ireland.

These developments were further confirmation that film had truly arrived at the centre of Irish culture. After six despairing years for many film-makers, the hopes and developments of 1981-87 can now be built on. For, while feature film production appeared to flourish during 1987–92, the reality was that the economic focus of Irish film production had largely shifted outside the country, overshadowing indigenous feature film production.

Feature Film Production

In recent years those feature films which have highlighted Ireland as a film production area have been almost exclusively funded from British and American sources. The Oscar-winning *My Left Foot* (1989) had more than 60 per cent of its IR£1.7 million budget invested by British televison, while the second feature from the same Irish producer/director team, *The Field* (1990), costing IR£4.5 million, was exclusively funded by British television. Similarly, *The Commitments* (1991), which cost $12 million, was British-directed and American-funded, *The Playboys* (1992), costing about $5 million, was directed by a Scot and funded from America, and the $50-$60 million blockbuster, *Far and Away* (1992), was also funded, as well as written, directed and largely crewed, by Americans. While these films bring in significant sums to Ireland by way of employment, spending on services, and taxation for the Irish exchequer, not all would be regarded as having made a significant contribution to an indigenous Irish film culture.

Though it is a UK/Ireland production, *The Crying Game* (1992) was also made in Britain, and its budget of about $4 million seems to have been provided mainly by British investors, after Neil Jordan had failed to convince Irish financiers to invest in it. Its enormous commercial success, especially in the United States, where its theatrical release alone took more than $60 million at the box-office, and its total income, after cable release and video sale and hire, could be as much as $100 million, has already made it the most commercially-successful foreign-produced film ever released in the US. However, little of this money will return to Ireland, with its UK production company and the American distributor, Miramax, receiving most of the income.

As the table below shows, over IR£52 million was spent in Ireland on live-action feature films during the five years 1987–91. The thirteen indigenous features made by independent producers had total budgets amounting to IR£23.2 million, while the fifteen off-shore productions spent an estimated IR£29.5 million in Ireland. The average budget size per production increased from IR£1.75 million in 1987 to IR£4.6 million in 1991. Closer scrutiny of the table is not possible, but it should be noted that the definition of an indigenous Irish film can be a moveable feast. While *My Left Foot* and *The Field*, as noted, were largely funded by foreign investors, the films are usually regarded as indigenous due to the fact that the films' creative contribution was largely Irish. As a result, the table should be treated with caution, as it is likely that off-shore investors contributed significantly more than IR£29.5 million of the IR£52.638 million listed.

VALUE OF LIVE-ACTION FEATURE FILM PRODUCTION

Year	Indigenous Productions	Off-Shore Productions	Value IR£Million
1987	2	5	12.271
1988	5	3	9.575
1989	3	1	6.504
1990	2	4	10.388
1991	1	2	13.900
TOTAL			52.638

Source: Coopers and Lybrand

During the interregnum between Bord Scannán Marks 1 and 2, the Irish Arts Council was the only statutory body giving grants to Irish film-makers. The sums allocated were quite modest, but they were often significant for aspiring film-makers in an otherwise bleak film landscape. While the Arts Council funded film organisations to the value of IR£524,000 during 1987–91, it only allocated a total of IR£410,000 for production during 1987–92, of which IR£100,000 was spent in 1992. Despite the small amounts available, interest in the Arts Council script awards grew from about sixty applicants in 1989 to 240 in 1992. Similar interest was expressed in the even more modest Film Base/RTE awards with only a few applicants in 1989 expanding to 120 in 1993. It is this tidal wave of film-making potential which the newly-constituted Bord Scannán will seek to harness.

While the Arts Council and Bord Scannán until now have allocated relatively modest sums to Irish film productions, RTE has, in total monetary terms, been of greater significance to independent film-makers. RTE occupies an anomalous but controversial position in Irish film production. With an annual budget of IR£120 million, it is by far the largest employer and investor in the Irish audio-visual sector. Yet, during the past fifteen years, it has singularly failed to develop its own television drama or to invest in co-productions with the independent sector in a manner analogous to Channel Four's *Film on Four* or the BBC's feature film projects. Its success in long-running soap operas, *Glenroe* and *Fair City*, has perhaps given RTE the illusion that this is 'drama' or 'fiction film'. The absence, in the 1980s, of RTE as interpreters, through drama, of a changing Irish society was a void which was filled by indigenous film-makers with the support of Bord Scannán and British television broadcasters, most especially Channel Four. As a consequence of this abdication of its public service responsibilities, RTE lost many defenders.

RTE has, of course, invested in independent production, but, while the figures may sound impressive, few film-makers are satisfied with the meagre amounts RTE pays for independent productions. The total value of the television sector, both Irish and British, to independent production was estimated at IR£6.7 million in 1991. Of this total, RTE invested $2.5 million. This was a decline from IR£3.1 million in 1990, though government restrictions on its income through the 'cap' on advertising revenue were blamed for this. Nevertheless, within the context of RTE's turnover of about IR£120 million, of which approximately half comes from television licence fees, these sums are small. During 1988–92, RTE commissioned an average of forty-four hours of documentaries and 104 hours of TV entertainment and magazine programmes per annum from the independent sector. No drama was commissioned. If the European directive, *Television Without Frontiers*, is fully implemented, RTE, like other EC television services, will be obliged to take 10 per cent of specialised programmes from the independent sector. The Minister's directive to RTE on commissioning from the independent sector will, it is hoped, ensure that this target is reached and that at least 20 per cent of total programming will come from the independent sector.

Independent Production Companies
The independent sector is certainly diverse and dynamic enough to respond to the new challenges. There are approximately 143 independent film production companies in the feature film and TV production areas, of which fifty account for the majority of productions. Another eight companies specialise in animation. Six further companies specialise in corporate video, while eleven make TV commercials. However, a closer look at one aspect of the

animation sector reminds us that the 'independent' is not immune from the familiar industrial/cultural dichotomy which is at the centre of the state's often limited approach to film production.

As a result of an active policy by the Industrial Development Authority to entice animation companies to establish production bases in Ireland, the value of the animation sector increased from IR£108,000 in 1987 to IR£19.1 million in 1991. Eighty-one per cent of this total was in animated feature film production. The most important of these animation companies was Sullivan-Bluth, later Don Bluth Entertainment, which accounted for 72 per cent of the employment in the sector until its demise in 1992. Its productions have included the animated feature *An American Tail* (1986). Don Bluth Entertainment had 370 staff when it began to experience cash flow difficulties and was eventually placed in liquidation. It was then taken over by a Hong Kong company, Media Assets, a subsidiary of Star TV, owner of Asia's largest satellite TV station, for $14 million, or 20 per cent of the cost of its productions. After Media Assets took over the company, about one-third of the workforce was retained. In August 1993, a majority shareholding in Star TV itself was bought by Rupert Murdoch's media conglomerate, thus putting a large section of Irish animation production in the hands of the owner of *The Sun*, a sure basis on which to build Irish film culture! These events suggest that Ireland's reliance on foreign investment in film, as elsewhere, is often built on ever shifting foundations. Indeed, the Bluth company saga is best understood in the context of an industrial policy which seeks to encourage foreign companies to invest in Ireland so as to take advantage of much cheaper labour than exists, in this case, in the highly organised American film industry. (The Bluth company would never have been accused of encouraging its employees to join trades unions, an approach to labour with which Mr Murdoch would undoubtedly concur.)

A close examination of the independent sector reveals that investment in indigenous independent film and television, out of which an Irish audio-visual culture is likely to emerge, is small. While the total value of the audio-visual 'industry' in 1990 was estimated at IR£62.052 million, only 26 per cent of this expenditure was on feature films and television productions. But, more crucially, 84 per cent of the expenditure in the film area, and 87 per cent in the area of television drama, came from outside

Ireland, thus illustrating once more the dependency on foreign investors in these critical cultural areas. While the Minister for Arts, Culture and the Gaeltacht has directed RTE to allocate more resources to independent film-makers, the measure of the effectiveness of the policy will be whether drama gets a significant share of the new monies. The evidence of recent years makes observers sceptical about the commitment of RTE to independently-produced drama and films. Its 1993 'breakthrough' into this area was to commission three half-hour dramas with a writers' brief that there could only be two characters in each programme. While the results overcame some of the brief's constraints, it was nonetheless a sad commentary on RTE's decline as a broadcasting institution. One can only hope for a more enlightened policy in the future.

Europe and Ireland
In an otherwise bleak situation, the EC's MEDIA programmes partly filled the void in Irish film production which occurred during 1987-93. There are nineteen MEDIA programmes (one of which, EVE, is based at the Irish Film Centre) which disperse funds to, and provide contacts and advice for, Irish film personnel at all levels. The value of much of this cannot be accurately quantified in monetary terms. For example, the brief of EURO AIM is to promote access to the market-place for independent producers and, while highly valued by Irish professionals, it is not a loan-giving or equity investment programme. Indeed, with the exception of SCALE, which is a programme dedicated to aiding production in smaller countries (Ireland, Greece, Benelux countries, Denmark), MEDIA programmes are precluded from investing directly in production, focusing principally on pre-production and post-production.

Due to its specific targeting, SCALE has become the largest provider of funds to Ireland, with about ECU400,000 in 1992. Next in financial importance is SCRIPT, which has had a key developmental role in supporting scriptwriting in recent years, and which was one of Bord Scannán's most important functions in the 1980s. SCRIPT's importance may be gauged from the statistics which reveal that it received eighty-seven Irish applications for funds in 1992. It supported fourteen of these with average sums of IR£15,000–IR£20,000, making it worth about IR£250,000 to Irish projects. Up to the end of 1991, SCRIPT had supported twenty-three Irish projects to a value of ECU378,376. In monetary terms, CARTOON has been the third most important project, while GRECO, which assists with marketing and distribution costs, has been the fourth. Overall, the value of MEDIA to Ireland up to the end of 1991 was about IR£1 million, while in 1992 alone it was in excess of ECU1 million, excluding EFDO's support for the theatrical release of the UK/Ireland production, *The Crying Game*. On a per capita basis, Ireland does very well from MEDIA. While Ireland accounts for about 1 per cent of the EC's population, it gets about 3 per cent of MEDIA's funding allocation, thus indicating both the quality of Irish projects and the commitment of a great many MEDIA programmes to indigenous productions.

MEDIA will continue to be critically important to Irish film professionals as even the most optimistic scenario after the re-establishment of Bord Scannán does not envisage more than one-third of the budget for any relatively large-scale Irish film being raised within Ireland. With the Board announcing that it will only provide up to 10 per cent of a film's budget as a loan or equity investment, a figure which is certain to be breached, the other key Irish investments, from RTE and Section 35, are not likely to bring the total Irish contribution to more than one-third for IR£1–4 million projects.

Along with MEDIA, the Eurimages programmes, involving twenty-three of the twenty-seven states of the Council of Europe, will help to fill the gap in production investment. Set up in 1988, Eurimages is a fund into which each member state pays an annual sum based on per capita GDP. Ireland's initial payment to the end of 1993 was IR£130,000 into a total Eurimages fund of $27.2 million. Co-productions must involve three partners, in this case independent producers from the Fund's member states. The first three awards to Irish producers went to Littlebird's *Rosaril* (with German and Dutch partners), Samson's *Talk of Angels* (with a Portugese lead producer and a German third partner), and Cinegael's *The Bishop's Story* (with a UK lead producer and a French partner). The value to the Irish producers of the Eurimages contribution for the first two projects was a total of IR£121,000, while the third received a total of IR£60,000.

Film Distribution and Exhibition

Film production is not the only sector which has been largely under foreign influence and control. Since the beginnings of cinema, Ireland and Britain have been considered as one territory for film distribution purposes. While some of the 'majors' have had offices in Dublin, all key decisions, including release dates for titles, have usually been taken in London. American and British films dominate the Irish market, a pattern which has existed since even before the advent of sound cinema, due to Ireland's use of the English language and its own limited film production. During 1986–90, an average of 70 per cent of the films released were American, 15 per cent were British, 2 per cent were Irish, and the other EC countries accounted for 6 per cent of the total.

However, there is compelling evidence that Irish audiences are keen to see more indigenous films. Irish-produced films were very popular in Ireland during the silent period but audiences have had few opportunities to see themselves represented in the cinema since. With the increase in Irish stories in the late 1980s and early l990s, the popularity of Irish films, irrespective of their cultural or artistic worth, has again been in evidence. Thus, in 1990, *The Field* became the first Irish-produced film, for which evidence exists, to top the box-office ratings. In the following year, *The Commitments* took IR£1.8 million at the box-office, rising to IR£2.2 million by the end of its run in 1992, making it the biggest ever Irish box-office hit. This trend continued in 1992. Despite the critical opprobrium heaped on them, *Far and Away* (1992) and *Patriot Games* (1992) were in the top ten, while the well-received *Into the West* (1992) was at number six. The success of these Irish-theme films in Ireland is encouraging and suggests that, if given the chance, Irish audiences will support indigenous film-making.

Conclusion

With the re-activation of Bord Scannán na hÉireann there is a chance to further dent the dominance of foreign cinema in Ireland, and the excessively influential role of foreign capital in films made about Ireland. This view is not being promoted as some negative form of cultural protectionism, as existed in the early decades of the Irish state, but rather as a positive assertion of the value of cinema as a significant cultural medium. The importance of such an approach can be usefully illustrated through the example of *The Field* which was exclusively funded by British television with guarantees of American distribution. It also illustrates most effectively the dilemma of a peripheral national culture such as Ireland's in the international arena.

Adapted from John B. Keane's play of the same name, the film contains two crucial changes from the play. The play is set in the late 1950s/early 1960s and is based on a real event. The film shifts the play's periodisation to the 1930s, thus discarding the film's potential for exploring Ireland during one of its most crucial conjunctures when it was changing from an inward-looking to an outward-looking society. Another important change is in the play's character of William Dee, played in the film by Tom Berenger. In the play, the character is a Galwayman who has been working in Britain, has become a successful businessman there, and who is returning to Ireland with his wife. Berenger's character is an Irish-American, a returned Yank, and as a consequence this dilutes the impact of the film. The contested issue of someone returning from Britain to buy land, with its sensitive historical resonances, would have had a greater cultural impact than that of a more neutrally-received Irish-American. These changes were made for quite particular reasons and were effectively forced on the production by the film's backers.

For many, Ireland in the cinema still retains an image of a pre-modern, pastoral society, something which the backers of *The Field* may have wished to trade on. To deal with 1960s Ireland would have required a confrontation with the modernisation of Irish society as well as an engagement with the conventional image of Ireland in the international cinema. The inclusion of American actor Berenger was a direct response to the long-standing requirement by foreign investors in Irish films to include even minor foreign stars in order to make Irish films palatable to American and British audiences. If the price of an Irish cinema in the past has been such compromises, then, it is to be hoped, that, in the new film cultural environment, such a dilution of indigenous cinema will be resisted and greater radicalism and experimentation amongst the younger Irish film-makers will be made possible.

NOTE

Some of the statistical data for this chapter was taken from the *Report on Indigenous Audiovisual Production Industry* (Dublin:1992) which was prepared by Coopers and Lybrand for the Irish Film Centre and Temple Bar Properties.

FILM PRODUCTION IN NORTHERN IRELAND

Geraldine Wilkins

The can be few places in Europe over the last twenty years or so, that have been more photographed, filmed or video-taped than Northern Ireland (NI). The protracted political crisis in NI, and the recurrence of the violence which accompanies this, has ensured that images of the region have appeared on the screens of the entire world, giving a global presence to a seemingly intractable local difficulty. And yet, for all its high media profile, very little of this imagery has emanated from the indigenous audio-visual industry itself. Northern Ireland's political difficulties might have given it a high media profile, but this has not changed the fundamentally peripheral status which NI endures in regard to Ireland, Britain and Europe. Rather, political uncertainty and instability have inevitably had an adverse effect on both NI's film industry and film culture.

As far as film production in NI is concerned, this peripherality was always the case and there has been relatively little film-making in the north over the years. Ireland's first sound film, *The Voice of Ireland* (1932), was in fact made in NI and it was followed by a short series of features starring the Northern Ireland singer and actor, Richard Hayward: *The Early Bird* (1936), *Irish and Proud of It* (1936), and *The Luck Of the Irish* (1937). These were, however, 'quota quickies' financed by Paramount in order to meet the requirements of the 1927 Films Act and did not lay the basis for a NI film industry. Northern Ireland continued to be used for some location work by a small number of British films (such as *Odd Man Out*, 1947 and *Jacqueline*, 1956) but no indigenous feature was made in Northern Ireland between the 1930s and the 1980s. During the 1980s the British film industry itself, lacking appropriate levels of government support, faced a production crisis.[1] It is not surprising, therefore, that in Northern Ireland this situation was mirrored, as in many other aspects of the NI economy, in a rather starker fashion.

This lack of an audio-visual infrastructure or support for production in Northern Ireland provoked the Independent Film, Video and Photography Association into commissioning a report, in the mid-1980s, on sources of funding for film and video in the region. The ensuing report, *Fast Forward*, published in 1988, compared policies and funding regimes for independent production in NI with other parts of the UK and the Republic of Ireland. The report highlighted the woeful lack of public sector support, and concluded that 'those areas which are best provided for in terms of film and video funding all have structures which have been formed as a result of progressive institutional or independent policies for the development of film and video'.[2] There was a clear need for an organisation that would address such issues, not only that of production funding, but also all the other elements necessary for the development of a culture of the moving image, such as training, media education, exhibition policies and archiving.[3]

Following on from this report, the Northern Ireland Film Council (NIFC), was set up in 1989. It was initially an unfunded voluntary organisation but, from 1992, it began to receive government support (via the Department of Education). The NIFC was set up as a representative body for both film and television and has been concerned to encourage the development and understanding of all aspects of film, television and video in the region.[4] The case for government funding for film was strengthened even further by the Priestley report on arts funding in the region. This report was particularly important as it put film and television formally on the arts agenda in NI for the first time, and also called on a newly reconstituted Arts Council to give more attention to film as an area of arts activity.[5] This is now set to happen with Arts Council support for film being routed through an independent Film Council.

As already indicated, the NIFC's concern has not been exclusively with film but also television. This is hardly surprising given the increasing inter-relations between the two. Television has moved from being a secondary buyer of completed films to playing a front-line role as a financier of movies. At the 1993 Cannes Film Festival, for example, fourteen of the the twenty-two films entered in the competition had some measure of television backing. Indeed, as Bertrand Moullier has indicated, terrestrial television now represents an average of twenty per cent of total revenue for the feature film industry world-wide (although this average conceals large variations from one territory to another).[6] This is a reflection both of the desire of the television companies to invest in film production and of the shortage of film finance from elsewhere. To put it bluntly, feature films need television, and television needs feature films.

It is worth remembering, however, that the reasons behind this trend have not only been commercial. In the UK, Channel Four's pioneering practice of investing in film was stimulated, in line with its special broadcasting remit, by cultural and artistic arguments. This encouragement of film has been in evidence not only in the drama department's support for the prestigious *Film on Four* but also in the work of the department of independent film and video. It was this department which, in the early 1980s, funded the workshops franchised under the *Workshop Declaration* and thus provided support to fledgling film-makers in NI. The first full-scale feature to be made under the *Workshop Declaration* was *Acceptable Levels* (1984) which was shot mainly in Belfast by Front-room Productions, in collaboration with Belfast Film Workshop. Its dramatisation of the story of an English television crew filming a documentary in Belfast was not only a challenging meditation upon the media's coverage of the 'troubles' but a rare example of local film-makers being provided with the opportunity to make a film about the political situation in the north from an insider's perspective. This was also true of *Hush-a-Bye Baby* (1989), made by Derry Film and Video, one of the two workshops in Northern Ireland to receive Channel Four support during the 1980s (Belfast Independent Video, now Northern Visions, was the other). Television has not only assisted work to be made but also to be seen. Indeed, *Hush-a-Bye Baby* had the highest viewing figures for any film screened in its particular broadcasting slot.

The track record of Channel Four, and also BBC 2, in investing in films for the small screen, some also intended for theatrical release, are rare examples in the UK context of support to the film industry. In other European Union (EU) countries, mechanisms for support from the television industry for film are more highly developed, and have government backing. In France, for example, terrestrial broadcasters are obliged to commit a minimum of three per cent of net annual turnover to film-related

development and production. In Britain and Ireland, to date, cinema has not yet enjoyed similar status as a cultural form (although there have been sporadic, and recently renewed, moves in that direction by governments in the Republic of Ireland).

To what extent is the influence of television cash – and television aesthetics – a damaging one for feature films? This is a hotly disputed issue – and one which I prefer to leave to film-makers and financiers. However, in the Northern Ireland context, a discussion of film production cannot ignore the role of the broadcasters, especially given the relative lack of government support for feature production in the UK generally and NI in particular. Local broadcasters have not so far been involved in supporting film features (except very modestly as in the case of Ulster Television's interest in *December Bride*, 1990). However, if BBC NI's drama productions (at least those shot in Northern Ireland) are taken into account, there is certainly some truth in the adage that 'of course there's a film industry here – it's called the BBC'. This is one of the many reasons why the current debate over BBC Charter renewal is so vital. For what is at stake is a large element of the regional industry infrastructure. *Extending Choice*, the BBC's response to the government's Green Paper, promises greater devolution of resources and decision-making to the BBC regions. What concerns many observers, however, is how this can be delivered at the same time as a continuing drive to cut costs across the Corporation – a process which tends towards centralisation and the economics of scale at the centre rather than the embracing of a new cultural agenda.[7]

On a more positive note the NIFC has established a Production Fund which will provide strategic support in two areas: development monies to enable projects to be brought to a point where they are able to attract production funding from other sources, and grants for the production of short films and videos. Small in scale it may be at this stage, but the NIFC's fund represents a significant breakthrough and is the first time that production resources will be available to film-makers with the specific but broadly defined remit of promoting a film and television culture in Northern Ireland.

This is admittedly an ambitious agenda but is it a sensible one? To what extent can one talk about a separate audio-visual culture of the north of Ireland? The relationship between film-makers in Northern Ireland to the industry in the Republic or to Great

Britain is the key to this question. The reference points for film-makers in NI tend to be south to Dublin, east to Scotland or south east to London. But even London is in reality only an outpost of a world industry dominated by Hollywood. Is the orientation of London necessary or helpful? It can be argued that the common language bonds between the US industry and London have actually hindered progress as undue emphasis is placed on the Hollywood model of film (and Hollywood budgets), rather than those found on continental Europe where scale, and hence costs, are more achievable.

In recent years there has been an increasing interest in the notion of 'Europe' as a point of political or cultural identification. Can films made in NI claim to be 'European'? They can now, at least, lay claim to European money, either through co-production or co-financing agreements with European broadcasters or financiers or via the public purse as recipients of MEDIA assistance. MEDIA is the EU programme set up to promote the development of an indigenous European film and television industry in the face of Hollywood's increasing domination. The NIFC is the local contact point for MEDIA projects, and gives information on the numerous, sometimes confusing, schemes operating under the MEDIA banner. Local producers should be able to benefit from their geographical/political position at the northern tip of the island by forging working links with producers in the Republic, thereby establishing potential co-production links without the barriers of language faced by most other European small country producers.

The latest developments in the film and television industry in the Republic of Ireland are also very exciting. A vigorous industry in the south, stimulated by government support, can only benefit writers, film-makers and crews across the island as a whole. More disappointing is the fact that films dealing with Northern Irish stories or themes, for instance Jim Sheridan's *In the Name of the Father* (1993), dealing with the Gerry Conlon story, continue to be shot outside the region. The Film Council is therefore working towards the establishment of a Screen Commission to make it easier for productions to be based here – whether film, TV or non-broadcast.

The rationale behind the Screen Commission is primarily commercial. However, for a small and economically vulnerable audio-visual industry, such as exists in NI, an increase in the use of

local technicians, actors and production facilities contributes towards the maintenance of the viable production base which is essential if indigeneous films, exploring and reflecting upon the complexity of society in Northern Ireland, are to emerge.

NOTES

1 For an overview of developments in the British film industry during the 1980s, see John Hill, 'Government Policy and the British Film Industry 1979–90', *European Journal of Communication*, vol. 8, no. 2, 1993.
2 *Fast Forward: Report on the Funding of Grant-aided Film and Video in the North of Ireland* (IFVPA: Northern Ireland, 1988), p.37.
3 For a discussion of the report and its implications see Martin McLoone, 'ACNI Culture: A Blurred Vision', *Circa*, no.39, 1988.
4 See Northern Ireland Film Council, *Strategy Proposals* (Northern Ireland,1991).
5 Clive Priestley, *Structures and Arrangements for Funding the Arts in Northern Ireland* (Department of Education: Northern Ireland, 1992).
6 Bertrand Moullier, 'Small Screen Bankrolls Big Picture', *Impact*, no. 7, 1993.
7 For a fuller discussion, see Martin McLoone, 'A Little Local Difficulty? Public Service Broadcasting, Regional Identity and Northern Ireland', in Sylvia Harvey and Kevin Robins (eds.), *The Regions, the Nations and the BBC* (British Film Institute: London, 1993).

NATIONAL CINEMA AND CULTURAL IDENTITY: IRELAND AND EUROPE

Martin McLoone

In the opening segment of his 1974 film *The Phantom of Liberty*, Luis Buñuel offers typically wry comment on what he sees as the ultimate absurdity of nationalism. The episode is set in Spain at the time of the Napoleonic invasion and provides a deliciously ironic re-working of Goya's heroic canvas *The Execution of the Defenders of Madrid*, painted in 1813.[1]

In Buñuel's version, a rather drab band of Spanish patriots has been rounded up by the French to face execution. As the firing squad prepares, one of their number shouts his final defiance of Napoleon's revolutionary message: 'Down with Liberty'. And he dies. For Buñuel, this is the *reductio ad absurdum* of nationalism – the desire to live with and die for the most reactionary, repressive regime in Europe rather than embrace 'foreign' ideas, no matter how liberating these might be.

This absurdity was for Goya a great personal dilemma. As a man of the Enlightenment, committed to the revolutionary principles of Liberty, Equality and Fraternity, Goya had a deep contempt for the hopelessly corrupt *ancien régime* of his native Spain. Like many liberal intellectuals of his day, he hoped that the revolutionary fervour from France would blow away corruption in Spain and with it the lingering vestiges of Inquisition Catholicism which sustained it. And yet when Napoleon's campaign in Spain provoked a surge of patriotic resistance, Goya was caught between his admiration for the French and his own burgeoning national pride.

Buñuel's mischievous re-working of Goya's dilemma raises in rather stark form a key dialectic in contemporary cultural debate – the dichotomy between the core and the periphery, between indigenous culture and cultural influences from outside. This dialectic is crucial to the construction of national or cultural identity and lies at the very centre of the nationalist project itself. And yet, it is an immensely more complex and contradictory relationship than has sometimes been allowed for within the didactic imperatives of cultural nationalism.

For nationalists, the cultural requirement has always been to establish a core set of characteristics, an essence, which defines the nation and gives cultural legitimacy to the political task of state-building. In Benedict Anderson's formulation, the nation is imagined as both 'inherently limited and sovereign'. Since, as Anderson continues, the nation can only be imagined against other entities, 'in the midst of an irremediable plurality of other nations', this imagining requires a process of sifting, of including and excluding, to establish these national limits.[2] In peripheral nation-building, then, the influences of economic and cultural centres are often rejected as 'foreign', no matter what the consequences.

Thus, underlying Buñuel's visualisation of Goya's dilemma there is a clear belief in the notion of a universal, progressive ideology, modernity itself, which both sustains and is nourished by the Enlightenment ideas which Goya propounded. What amuses and angers Buñuel is that his native Spain rejected modernity as a 'foreign' imposition and withdrew into an anti-modernist culture sustained by a repressive and superstitious Catholicism. Indeed, this repressive culture is a recurring motif throughout his film-making career and is the central influence which he identifies in his autobiography.[3]

Buñuel's ridiculing of essentialist nationalism is very pertinent today, given that the core/periphery dichotomy is once again at the centre of contemporary cultural debate. However, the emphasis today is no longer solely on peripheral cultures and peripheral nation-building. Even a few years ago, it might have seemed perverse to include a former imperial power like Britain in a discussion about national cultures under threat. It might have appeared even more incongruous to include a multinational conglomerate of former imperial powers like Europe in such debate. But today this is common. In a rather amused comment on current debates about national cinemas, Julio Garcia Espinosa, formerly head of ICAIC, the Cuban Film Institute, observes:

Almost a 100 years ago Latin America began calling out in the wilderness, declaring its right to make films. The only thing to have happened is that after a 100 years Western Europe also declared its right to make films. Today it turns out that an English film is just as exotic as a film from Ecuador . . . Today we are witnessing the unexpected, as the problem of national culture ceases to be a concern only of Third World countries.[4]

I detect here a certain amount of glee at the historic irony of Europe's (and England's) predicament, though to be fair to Espinosa he is motivated more by shared experience and shared loss than he is by bitterness or rancour. As he argues, 'Yesterday, Latin America asked for Europe's solidarity. It still does, but it also offers solidarity to Europe'.[5]

Behind Espinosa's argument lies the spectre of the USA and the seemingly total supremacy of Hollywood cinema on a global scale. The consequent collapse of Europe's national cinemas is not only a great loss in itself but it raises doubts about the very idea of a national cinema in the first place. For if the formerly powerful nation-states of Europe can no longer sustain national film cultures, what hope is there for the Third World? Espinosa, rightly I think, raises the possibility of transnational solutions to national problems – Ecuador within Latin America, England within Europe – but, perhaps not surprisingly, he misses some of the subtle ironies within the European (and British) situation.

For if Latin America has been 'calling out in the wilderness for a hundred years, declaring its right to make films', then within Europe so have a host of less visible and more peripheral nations and states, including, of course, Ireland.[6] Indeed, the debate about national culture has been almost a constant in Ireland since the 1840s, pre-dating the birth of cinema and covering every aspect of cultural production since. In this regard then, Espinosa is mistaken to link, until relatively recently, the debate about national culture to only the Third World. In fact, this debate has flourished in the 'first world' (for example, in the Celtic periphery of Europe) but was generally regarded as a rather archaic relic of pre-modern times, an irrelevant side-show to the onward march of modernity and progress.

A number of factors coincided to change this. First, in the political arena, the accelerating pace of European integration within the EC gave rise to wider debates about regional, national and supranational identities. Second, the sweeping changes in

Eastern Europe at the end of the 1980s and the collapse of the Soviet Union in 1991 re-kindled the ethnic nationalism and ethnic conflicts held in check by state communism. Finally, in the cultural sphere, the world-wide success of *Dallas* in the 1980s seemed to symbolise the total dominance of the American audio-visual industries throughout the globe and gave a renewed urgency to questions about national cultures everywhere. The irony is that Ireland's own local difficulties are now being played out in a larger arena (where even the tragedies of violent conflict in Northern Ireland are mirrored on a larger scale in the ethnic wars of Eastern Europe). Ireland's long and continuing preoccupation with questions of national culture are, therefore, peculiarly relevant to these wider cultural debates and Ireland's negotiation of core/periphery relationships is particularly instructive to current debates in Europe about the idea of a national cinema.

National Culture, Globalisation and Modernity

On 25 November 1892, just a few years before the birth of cinema, the future President of Ireland, Douglas Hyde, delivered a speech in Dublin which was to influence profoundly the nature of Irish cultural nationalism. Hyde's address on 'The Necessity for De-Anglicizing Ireland' was premised on the conviction that what was *essentially* Irish was the Gaelic language and the ancient Gaelic heritage of the Irish people. He argued that '. . . within the last ninety years we have, with unparalleled frivolity, deliberately thrown away our birthright and anglicized ourselves . . . ceasing to be Irish without becoming English'.[7]

Regardless of Hyde's original intentions, his formulation was to become the central plank in Irish cultural nationalism for the next sixty years, creating in the process the kind of insular, xenophobic and anti-modernist culture in Ireland which Buñuel would have recognised only too well. Indeed, the only country which rivalled Catholic Ireland in terms of strict censorship laws, aimed at both literature and cinema, was Catholic Spain of the same period.[8] The prevailing ethos, as Kevin Rockett has demonstrated, was inimicable to the cinema as an institution and to film as an art form.[9] The result of this was a curious set of paradoxes that are worth considering in some detail for what they might tell us about the wider problematic – the role of indigenous film culture within an increasingly global popular cinema.

The first result was, of course, that no film industry developed in Ireland and no infrastructural support for a film culture was forthcoming from successive Irish governments. Thus, echoing Espinosa's rhetorical flourish, the cinematic voice cried out in the wilderness unheard. And yet, the first paradox is that, given the narrowness of the official national culture, and the poverty of the national imagining, perhaps one can be forgiven for thinking that this was no bad thing in the end. Given the prevailing cultural climate in Ireland, right down to the 1960s, can we envisage a state-funded national cinema that would have had any real cultural value, or one that would have accommodated alternative, sceptical or oppositional voices? Indeed, one of Ireland's more tireless campaigners for a national film industry was a Jesuit priest Fr. Richard Devane SJ, who is reported as saying in 1939 'There is no greater material gift from God to man than the cinema properly used'.[10]

In such a conservative, Catholic culture as this, there was no shortage either of official comment on the cinema when it was perceived to have been improperly used. In 1937, for example, Bishop MacNamee of Ardagh and Clonmacnoise is quoted as saying:

> The emigration of young girls to Great Britain: they are lured perhaps, by the fascinations of the garish distractions of the city, and by the hectic life of the great world as displayed before their wondering eyes in the glamorous unrealities of the films ... For it is not the least of the sins of the cinema to breed a discontent that is anything but divine in the prosaic placidity of rural life ...[11]

This raises a second paradox about the nature of the cinema experience in Ireland. By the early 1930s, because there were no indigenous Irish films to compete, Ireland's screens were dominated by mainly American films to a greater extent than those of most other countries in Europe. And yet, in a climate where the official culture was so repressive, these 'foreign' images became positively life-enhancing. As Kevin Rockett has argued:

> Despite ... the severity of Irish film censorship ... especially from the 1920s to the 1950s, it is probably true that Hollywood cinema provided an attractive and perhaps liberating alternative to official ideologies.[12]

These sentiments are echoed by Geoffrey Nowell-Smith in relation to British culture as well. Compared to their American counterparts, he argues, British films appeared to be 'restrictive and stifling, subservient to middle-class artistic models and to middle and upper-class values'.[13] This is a paradox which continues to be relevant not just in Ireland, but right across the globe wherever Hollywood cinema has gained an ascendancy. Many reasons have been adduced for the pleasures which Hollywood cinema gives to so many diverse cultures. Duncan Webster, for example, has argued that American culture in general has a more democratic mode of address, having emerged originally from the melting pot of so many diverse immigrant cultures. American culture is not monolithic, in other words, but is plural in its construction and open in its address. It is now anyway, part of Europe's own popular culture and American images, icons and genres can themselves be employed to explore aspects of European cultural identity.[14]

Hollywood cinema, then, has insinuated its way into the consciousness of Ireland, Britain and Europe so completely that its images are now part of common currency. However, there is in the Irish example yet another paradox which needs to be considered. In a situation where Hollywood cinema has dominated the screens of Ireland unchallenged by indigenous film-making, the only cinematic images of Ireland with which the Irish were familiar were the representations that flowed out of the Hollywood industry (and at crucial points when it was productive, the British industry as well). In other words, 'cinematic Ireland' was entirely a foreign construction. As Rockett, Gibbons and Hill argue:

> Due to the Irish state's failure to provide for a native film industry . . . popular representations of Ireland on the screen have . . . been left to the predominantly commercial designs of American and British companies . . . Ireland's peripheral (and ex-colonial) status has not simply hampered the possibilities for a native film industry but, in its absence has also made possible a set of cinematic representations which have tended to sustain a sense of cultural inferiority.[15]

This is particularly disabling, Hill goes on to argue, when these cinematic images work against an understanding of Irish politics and society and especially of the nature of political violence in Ireland.[16] Thus it is important that indigenous representations are encouraged, both to challenge the primacy of the outsider's view but more importantly to establish an alternative set of images to these dominant representations.

This brings us back, of course, to a problem similar to that identified in 1892 by Douglas Hyde. Indeed, one might sum up the centenary of the cinema in Ireland by slightly rewording Hyde's original claim: '. . . within the last ninety years we have, with unparalleled frivolity, deliberately thrown away our birthright and Los Angelesised ourselves . . . ceasing to be Irish without becoming American'. Formulated in this way, the claim would now look familiar to J.G. Espinosa in Cuba and would rally a great deal of support across Europe.

By following through on these paradoxes in the Irish experience we have arrived at seemingly contradictory conclusions. On the one hand, a brief survey of Irish cultural nationalism would seem to demonstrate the inherent danger in the nationalist project, the danger of an essentialist definition of cultural identity which is stifling in its narrowness and oppressive in its lack of generosity. Equally, this essentialism can thwart the process of modernity itself, by insisting on some kind of primeval purity which denies all that is positive, progressive and enlightened in the more powerful 'foreign' culture.

And yet the Irish experience also clearly shows the repressive and suffocating tendencies of dominant, metropolitan culture. This is the problem of cultural imperialism, the colonisation of the unconscious, in which, to adapt Albert Memmi's formulation, the colonised culture can finally only recognise itself in the image promoted in the first instance by the colonising culture itself. As Memmi has argued in relation to 'native-settler' relationships:

> Constantly confronted with this image of himself, set forth and imposed on all institutions and in every human contact, how could the colonized help reacting to his portrait? It cannot leave him indifferent and remain a veneer which, like an insult, blows with the wind. He ends up recognizing it as one would a detested nickname which has become a familiar description. The accusation disturbs him and worries him even more because he admires and fears his powerful accuser.[17]

It is something of this process which John Hill has detected in ostensibly Irish films like *Angel* (1982) and *Cal* (1984), which, in their portrayal of violence in Ireland, end up reinforcing dominant British representations of Ireland and the Irish.[18]

The paradoxes of Irish cultural nationalism in its relationship to the cinema confirm, to my mind, the original dilemma which faced Goya – a choice between a self-defeating essentialism and a self-abusing domination. Following Wallerstein, Roland Robertson describes this dilemma in terms of the ambiguous desire for assimilation into a *universal* while at the same time adhering to a *particular*. This universalism/particularism issue, for Robertson, is a central problematic in the whole question of 'globalisation'.[19]

Indeed, even the essentialist thrust of Douglas Hyde's nationalism is a manifestation of this, for what Hyde proposed was that a recognisably *particular* Gaelic/Irish nation should take its place within a *universal* network of other nations (of other particularities). Thus, what Hyde desired, his own form of particularism/universalism, was not the problem in itself. Rather, the shortcoming in his own thesis was that he felt that, to achieve its own identity, Ireland needed to divest itself of all manifestations of the other particularities that made up this universal network. But, as Robertson argues, universalism/particularism is an inter-penetrating discourse. Using Japan as his example, he elaborates:

> Japan's crystallization of a form of 'universalistic particularism' since its first encounter with China has resulted in its acquiring paradigmatic, global significance with respect to the handling of the universalism-particularism issue. Specifically its paradigmatic status is inherent in its very long and successful history of selective incorporation and syncretization of ideas from other cultures in such a way as to particularize the universal and, so to say, return the product of that process to the world as a uniquely Japanese contribution to the universal.[20]

Hyde's assertion that the Irish had ceased to be Irish without becoming English was, thus, beside the point. 'Irishness' was, and is, deeply penetrated by other influences (especially, of course, English) but this is the universal condition of all particularities (or nations). Identity is a dynamic process, not a fixed point, and part of the process is the assimilation of, and thus the changing of, outside influences. In Robertson's formulation, the twentieth century has witnessed 'a massive, twofold process involving the interpenetration of the universalization of particularism and the particularization of universalism'.[21]

Robertson's formulation grows out of a discourse about 'globalisation' and surely we need just such a notion if we are to contain, within the same discourse, the cultural problems of Ireland and Ecuador or indeed of England, Europe and Latin America. But there still remains the key concept which underlies the notion of globalisation, the question of *modernity*, which was rejected by Hyde, lamented by Goya and the absence of which motivated Buñuel's sense of the absurd.

John Tomlinson has argued that the broader discourse of cultural imperialism is in fact a discourse about *the spread of the culture of modernity itself*:

> This is a discourse of historical change, of 'development', of a global movement towards, among other things, an everyday life governed by the habitual routine of commodity capitalism. One reason for calling this discourse a broader one is that the 'imaginary' discourse of cultural identity only arises *within* the context of modernity.[22]

Thus, resistance to what is perceived as 'cultural imperialism' is often a critique of urban industrial capitalism itself, especially of its consumerist thrust and its tendency towards homogenisation. In this regard then, Hollywood's increasingly global dominance has become the symbol of American economic might and resistance to Hollywood is a cultural challenge to the hegemony of American capital.

However, I think that this, too, is a simplification of the core/periphery relationship. For in the discourse of globalisation, the 'core' is the global system of multinational and transnational capitalism. The centre is, therefore, everywhere and nowhere in particular. It is in New York, Tokyo, London and Frankfurt, but it is also in the financial districts of Dublin and Quito. In the discourse of globalisation, we are all, at the same time, part of both the periphery and the core.

Of course, some nations, states and peoples are closer to the centre than others and within these same nations, states and peoples, some groups or classes are themselves more central than others. Modernity, historical change or 'development' has had an unequal growth. In its global spread this has created inequalities and injustices in the exploitation of human and physical resources. These contradictions are addressed most directly in the political arena. Indeed, the former Soviet Union can now be seen as an experiment in negotiating modernity outside the terms set by the dynamic of capitalism. Its failure may have given this dynamic an unchallenged position globally, but it has not removed the political need to address modernity's contradictions.

Thus, for example, the Irish experience of modernity clearly demonstrates the problems and the dangers which lie in either rejecting modernity or in embracing it wholeheartedly. The Irish experience with Hollywood cinema equally shows the contradictions in the culture of modernity. On one hand, as we have seen, Hollywood offers real pleasures that have allowed it to insinuate its way into national consciousness and on the other hand, left unchallenged, it has colonised this consciousness completely.

It seems to me, then, that modernity is the key concept in the universalism/particularism dichotomy and is the catalyst which energises core/periphery relationships. Identity is formed, therefore, at the interface of modernity's contradictions. Indeed, I want to argue that national identity is the social imagining which results from the conditions under which modernity interacts with a particularity. The fissures and flux of cultural identity result from the demands which modernity makes of a particular nation but also from the negotiations with modernity which this particular nation itself makes. This is the fundamental dialectic, a dialectic *pas de deux* which influences greatly the cultural domain. Thus, if Hollywood cinema has become the cultural symbol of modernity's universalising discourse, then national cinema should be a response to this, a manifestation of the demands, the conditions and the negotiations involved in a national culture's relationship to Hollywood.

I have been arguing that the particularism/universalism formulation allows us to understand better the paradoxes of Ireland's relationship to the cinema and to grasp the real significance of the dilemma which is posed by them. Furthermore, this formulation allows a way through the problems of theorising what a 'national' cinema might be, or could be, within the 'universal' paradigm of Hollywood. I want now to consider in some detail the films which have emerged from within Ireland, north and south, over the last twenty years or so. Though relatively small in number, and constrained by low (sometimes miniscule) budgets, I believe that this body of work represents the beginnings of a recognisably indigenous film industry, the tantalising outline to a genuine Irish national cinema, which has begun the process of re-imagining Ireland's relationship to modernity.

'Critical Regionalism' and Film in Ireland

The turning point for film production in Ireland was the 1973 Arts Act.[23] For the first time, film was recognised as an art form which was eligible for state funding. In 1977 the Arts Council formalised its support for film production by establishing an annual script award, putting in place, finally, the first ever state funding mechanism for film production.

The next two decades can usefully be considered as three historical periods. The first, from 1973–1981, was a period of slow growth, stimulated by the Arts Council and fuelled by the emergence of an effective film lobby of independent producer/ directors. The result was an accomplished group of (mainly short) films and the establishment in 1981 of Bord Scannán na h-Éireann, The Irish Film Board (BSE).

The second phase, from 1982–87, covers the years of BSE's existence. This period was marked by a steady output of feature-length fiction films and a growing sense of optimism about the future. This phase ended abruptly when the government shut down Bord Scannán in 1987.

The third period, from 1987–93, covers the years of anger and pessimism as the film lobby in Ireland regrouped and relaunched a campaign for state funding. Finally, in 1993, Bord Scannán was re-established and one assumes that a new period of growth and optimism has begun. The ironic aspect of this third period is, however, that while it became almost impossible for indigenous films to be made, Irish themes became more attractive to American and British film-makers, culminating in a flurry of films made in or about Ireland. The success of *My Left Foot* (1989), which won Best Actor and Best Supporting Actress Oscars in 1990, is credited with stimulating this interest in Ireland and the subsequent box-office or critical success of *The Field* (1990), *The Commitments* (1991), *Patriot Games* (1992) and *The Crying Game* (1993) has kept this interest going.

A second irony about this third period is that it also witnessed an unprecedented growth in short film-making, coming in the main from the graduates of Dun Laoghaire School of Art and Design and Rathmines College, completing short film projects as part of their studies. Short film-making also received a boost from a range of short-film/script awards established by various bodies during these years and the consequent improvement in technical skills and expertise was both obvious and very welcome.

These undoubtedly positive developments nonetheless only highlight more the fact that, without the support of state funding, it had become almost impossible to fund major indigenous productions during this period. In this regard then, the achievements of the first two periods appear now to have been quite substantial and provide a benchmark against which the developments in the third period might be contrasted.

It is hardly surprising that when this recognisably indigenous body of films began to emerge in Ireland from the mid-1970s on, it demonstrated a critical engagement with the legacy of Irish cultural nationalism. Thus, a coherent set of overlapping themes can be detected:

–an interrogation of the rural mythology which underpinned cultural nationalism and is encapsulated in the use of landscape;
–a new concern to represent urban experience which was largely submerged and ignored by this rural mythology;
–a consequent desire to reveal the social and political failures of independent Ireland;
–an interrogation of religion in Ireland, especially in relation to education and sexuality;
–an interrogation of Irish history and Irish tradition, especially the manner in which these have been used to construct notions of identity;
–the question of women in Ireland, especially in relation to nationalist rhetoric, Catholic teaching and imagery, and the discourse around women's bodies;
–the question of Northern Ireland, political violence and the disputed notions of identity which form the crux of the conflict;
–overall, an assessment of the discourse of Irish nationalism and its continuing dominance over political and social discourse in

Ireland, and especially its relationship to progress and modernisation.

Finally, and again not surprisingly, given that 'cinematic Ireland' has been dominated by Hollywood or British images, indigenous film-making has attempted to explore film form itself, in an attempt both to destabilise dominant imagery and to construct a different film language, one that is adequate to the films' thematic explorations.

These themes began to emerge in a remarkable group of short films produced independently in the 1970s and funded from a variety of sources. In 1975, Bob Quinn's *Caoineadh Airt Ui Laoire (Lament for Art O'Leary)* marked something of a breakthrough for indigenous film-making.[24] Indeed, Quinn's film was the first independent fiction film produced in Ireland since Tom Cooper's non-professional feature *The Dawn*, made in 1936. Furthermore, it was the first ever Irish language fiction film to be produced independently. The film tackles some of the key elements in Irish cultural nationalism, including the cultural significance of the west of Ireland, the Irish language itself and Irish history and tradition and explores the way in which these impinge on contemporary Ireland.

The film is based on the Irish lament of the same name, written in the 1770s by O'Leary's widow after her husband died in a confrontation with an English landlord. However, the lament itself is the centre of a complex set of representations – a poem within a film, within a play, within a film. A group of actors rehearse a play based on the poem. This play employs a series of filmed inserts, shot as a costumed fiction based on the poem's events. Interwoven into this complex, the play's actors discuss their own filmic portrayals and argue historical interpretations with the play's director (played by English playwright, John Arden).

This complex structure raises issues of representation and presents history not as a given set of irrefutable facts, but as a question of representation, a matter of interpretation which is used to meet the ideological needs of the present. At the centre of the film is a debate over the courageous acts of violence represented by the historic Art O'Leary's confrontation with English authority and the significance that these have for the continuing tradition of militant nationalism in Northern Ireland.

The film was funded by Sinn Féin, The Workers' Party at a crucial point in that organisation's development away from radical nationalist politics to the more socialist views espoused by the party (Democratic Left) that it evolved into in the 1990s. It is a key cinematic statement of a time of reappraisal and reassessment, of a period when the rapid process of modernisation, undertaken in the 1960s, seemed to reach its culmination in 1972 when Ireland's entry into the EC was given an overwhelming endorsement in a referendum. The film's re-negotiation of key elements in Irish nationalism, no matter how tentative they look in retrospect, nonetheless pointed forward to a dominant theme in subsequent films.

In its complex formal structure, its mixing of different modes of representation, the film establishes what later emerged as another key element in indigenous Irish films – the exploration of film language itself. The film's director, Bob Quinn, continued to contribute important, questioning films throughout the three periods I have identified, creating in the process a formidably eccentric and challenging body of work which not only explores the myths that bound together the traditional discourses of cultural nationalism, but which also offers an acerbic critique of the 'modernity' which threw this into crisis in the first place.

Thus, *Poitín* (1978) offers a deliberately unromantic view of the west of Ireland which, in cultural nationalism, was the repository of those Gaelic, rural values which were to be the basis of Ireland's anti-modernist utopia. In his three-part television documentary, *Atlantean* (1983), Quinn scrutinises the whole Celtic mythology in Ireland in an ironic and absurdist manner by arguing the case for the Irish being descended from North African Arab sea-farers. In *Budawanny* (1986), Quinn returns to the west of Ireland to explore the clash between the formal, organised structures of the Catholic Church and a more pagan or elemental form of religion which the people themselves adhere to. The clash is precipitated by a priest who lives in the remote Clare Island parish with his housekeeper. When she becomes pregnant he seeks the bishop's consent to pursue his priestly duties regardless.

Quinn's work is witty and ironic, constantly undermining its own seriousness and pretensions with a built-in leavening of humour. His films exist in an ironic relationship with both tradition and modernity, on one hand castigating cultural nationalism's use, or abuse, of Gaelic Ireland while at the same time, being deeply suspicious of the modernity represented by Dublin (and Hollywood). In lamenting the adoption by Gaeltacht school children of what he calls 'Dallas-speak', Quinn has been a vociferous advocate for the establishment of an Irish language television service. As he has said, 'Otherwise the children of the Gaeltacht will continue replacing the language of their parents with the dialects of Bill Cosby and Kylie Minogue'.[25] Quinn's ambivalence to both cultural nationalism and modernity is emblematic of the whole contradictory interface between the particular and the universal which I have attempted to delineate. His films offer no final resolutions, indeed pretend to no definitive statements. But in their scepticism, irony, and self-deflating humour, they offer important instances of the kind of conditional negotiation with tradition and modernity which is characteristic of the best indigenous films.

Joe Comerford is another director who, despite the difficulties, has managed to sustain his film-making career throughout the last two decades. After a number of short films made in the 1970s, Comerford has since made three feature length films of considerable importance – *Traveller* (1982), *Reefer and the Model* (1988) and *High Boot Benny* (1993). Comerford established his importance with his 1978 short film *Down the Corner*, which was financed by the British Film Institute. *Down the Corner* is set in the working-class Dublin estate of Ballyfermot and marks a considerable milestone in the cinematic project of giving voice and image to the urban working-class. The opening sequences of urban industrial Dublin, scenes shot in a foundry, are a remarkable departure in cinematic imagery of Ireland, establishing the missing discourse of the city almost for the first time. The film was shot using a local, non-professional cast and taps into a naturalistic tradition of film-making which was common in Britain though rare in Ireland.

The critique of urban living is a familiar one. Through a series of vignettes, the film establishes the effect of urban poverty on a group of young boys; the lack of opportunity, unemployment, irrelevant schooling and the kind of cheek-by-jowl living conditions which lead to family bickering. Visually, the film establishes the confinement that the boys' lives entails, with claustrophobic shots of fenced in back-yards and small kitchens. Dogs growling on either side of the fence symbolise the family bickering which results from this confinement. The film's sympathy with these marginalised young people is echoed in Comerford's later portrayals of the marginalised and the dispossessed in the feature films which followed, but two other aspects of *Down the Corner* are worth mentioning.

Although the film is primarily concerned with portraying the urban working-class with sympathy and understanding, Comerford nonetheless is aware that to do so is to engage in a dialogue with the rural cultural nationalism which underpinned the foundation of the state. In one sequence, the boys climb over a high, barbed wire-protected wall to rob an orchard. This escape from the urban to the rural brings both discourses together in a productive tension, one which is brought to a head when one of the boys badly cuts his foot on broken glass. The environmental hazards of urban living have impinged on the rural, necessitating the boy's visit to the inadequate medical attention of a inner urban hospital. As a metaphor for the failed rural utopia, the film works well enough on this level, but a second remarkable sequence considerably confuses the issue.

In a black and white insert sequence the grandmother of one of the boys narrates an incident from the War of Independence, in which she and her boyfriend, on the run from the British authorities, were forced to kill a British soldier. The scene is intensely ambiguous. Does it allude to the contemporary situation in the North? Is it a reminder of the heroic sacrifices that once were made on behalf of Irish freedom but which were betrayed by a state which today tolerates such urban deprivation? Does it intimate that the armed struggle fought then was irrelevant to the urban working-class or perhaps that the armed nationalist struggle in Northern Ireland today is irrelevant to real social issues?

As with Bob Quinn's films, Comerford's work is always ambiguous and eliptical, but whereas Quinn's ambiguity is a result of his own deep irony, Comerford's results from the severity of his vision. He is most interested in the totally marginalised and dispossessed in society, (an earlier short, *Withdrawal*, 1974, dealt with heroin addicts) and these severe victims of modernity's inequalities give Comerford's cinema a cold bleakness. Indeed, his films are lowly (as opposed to highly) stylised, probing at the edges of society with an angst which eschews embellishment. His feature films, *Traveller* and *High Boot Benny* in particular, are narratively disjointed and confusing, mirroring the dysfunctional confusion of the main characters.

Comerford's films are always deeply metaphorical, so that his marginalised characters and oblique narratives can be read as symbolic motifs of contemporary Ireland. Thus, the travellers in *Traveller* are both the forgotten victims of progress, but also can be read as a metaphor for the dispossessed nationalist people of the North. The dysfunctional families in *Down the Corner, Reefer and the Model* and the perverse family grouping in *High Boot Benny* are all metaphors for the sickness of the nation itself.

Comerford's bleak imagining of the nation is a result of what he sees as the unfulfilled idealism of Irish nationalist rhetoric. No other southern film-maker has engaged with Northern Ireland and its continuing significance so completely as he has. No other film-maker has explored the gap between the high idealism of Irish nationalism and the sick and sorry state of contemporary Ireland in the way he has.

This is most evident in *High Boot Benny*. Comerford here creates his most emphatically bleak vision of Ireland (the film was shot in the Inishowen peninsula of Donegal in mid-winter) which challenges visually the dominant romantic imagery of Irish landscape. Indeed it is difficult to enjoy this scenery for its own sake, for behind every rock, and just over every hill, one feels the presence of masked military or paramilitary gunmen engaged in a incoherent and inconclusive bloodbath (blood, entrapment and death permeate the film). This is a nightmarish border community of the imagination, Comerford's most complete vision of the dysfunctional nation which he sees is a result of the bleeding sore that is Northern Ireland.

There is, though, in Comerford's vision, a deep and genuine human sympathy for these marginalised and largely inarticulate characters. In *Reefer and the Model*, Comerford offers a new imagining of the nation in the constructed family of outcasts which he assembles – the Model herself, no exemplar of traditional values, is a pregnant ex-prostitute and drug addict, recently returned from London. Badger is gay, Spider is an IRA man from the North who is on the run and who has lost faith in the cause (at one point he admits to having only joined in the first place to attract the girls) and Reefer is an eccentric mix of Walter Mitty, petty criminal, west-coast adventurer and fireside republican.

Comerford's challenging vision of Ireland's identity crisis poses extreme problems for the audience. His adherence to a naturalistic aesthetic (his films, for example, feature many non-professional actors in main parts) and his narrative disjunctions are at odds with dominant realist forms, especially, of course, the high-octane narratives of Hollywood. To that extent, his film language is engaged in a debate with dominant forms anyway.

However, what is remarkable about *Reefer and the Model* is that he builds into his visual style and narrative construction a stylistic inner-dialogue about film-making itself. Thus, the film employs two styles – an austere, European art cinema aesthetic, which is his own preferred style, and a pastiche of the Hollywood chase movie. Both styles of course are rendered problematic in their encounter with Irish stereotypes and the west of Ireland scenery. In this clash of styles and traditions, everything is changed and the resultant vision is one of amusing, and bemusing, strangeness.

The most subversive aspect of *Reefer and the Model* is the scene in the pub on the Aran island ('The American Bar') in which Badger dances with, gently fondles and then kisses his male lover during the ceilidh. Like the Model's perverse image of women, Badger's homosexuality is both a sign of the film's concern with the marginalised and the despised in society, but also a challenge to the dominant ideologies of cultural nationalism and Irish Catholicism. This concern with male sexuality is alluded to in two other remarkable short films of this first period, Kieran Hickey's *Exposure* (1978) and Cathal Black's *Our Boys* (1981).

Exposure ends with a photographic exposure in a darkroom – three men, smiling, framed against the wildness of a west of Ireland setting, arms around each other in a pose typical of male camaraderie. The youngest in the middle is supported by the two older men on either side. The photographer then switches on the light and the exposure fades. This photograph is the key image in the film and the narrative sets out to probe the connotations of the image, to expose the reality of male camaraderie and Irish masculinity.

The three men meet Caroline, a French photographer, in an out-of-season hotel in the west of Ireland while they are on a surveying job and she on a photographic assignment. The older man, Dan, is middle-aged with a grown-up son and a failing marriage, the second man, Eugene, is newly married with a young baby and the youngest, Oliver, is single. But this is really the same man, at different stages in his life, the Irish male, educated in a sexually repressive Catholic culture and unable to sustain

onships with women. Indeed, this composite
norant of women he is threatened by women's
ndependence. When Oliver strikes up a
Caroline, the other two withdraw into surly
drunkenness. a scene of immensely disturbing power, the
drunken Dan and Eugene break into Caroline's bedroom when
she is out with Oliver. They rummage through her belongings and
play pathetically with her underwear in a scene of shocking
symbolic rape. Their rage is the rage of the deeply misogynist,
their incoherence that of those who have slipped out of rational
discourse and into the heart of darkness.

When Caroline and Oliver arrive, all three men return to their
rooms, unable to face Caroline's bewilderment. Oliver's liberated
relationship was short-lived and he is drawn, once more, into the
self-hating and suffocating male camaraderie of Catholic Ireland.
Exposure is a powerfully wrought fable of sexual and social
oppression, an acerbic riposte to the image of Irish male pub
camaraderie much beloved of film-makers like John Ford. The
composite Irish male of Kieran Hickey's film is a long way from the
amiable drunkenness of a Victor McLaglen.

The question of Catholic repression is the subject matter of
perhaps the finest of these short films, Cathal Black's *Our Boys*
(1981). Black's film is emblematic and important for a number of
reasons. Its completion at all is a triumph of will over adversity. It
took over three years to make, costing in total a mere £5,200, a
paltry sum even in 1981. The film stock and the finance were
cobbled together from a number of sources, including RTE, the
Arts Council of Northern Ireland and BSE. The film was shot in
periodic bursts of activity as these became available.

Our Boys garnered great praise when it was released in the
Autumn of 1981, eventually winning an award at the Melbourne
Film Festival. And then, inexplicably, having helped to produce it,
RTE declined to show the film for ten years, finally relenting in
February 1991. This amounted to censorship, of course, and is
testament to the film's power to challenge, disturb and provoke. It
also highlights one of the major problems which faces a national
cinema, especially a cinema which sets out to explore as well as to
entertain – the problem of distribution and exhibition.

This is not a uniquely Irish problem. Writing about Australian
cinema, Susan Dermody and Elizabeth Jacka point out the
obvious, but nonetheless, often forgotten reality:

Local distribution and exhibition are vital to local production, but local production is still relatively incidental to the local film trade.[26]

When, as is the case with *Our Boys*, the local public service broadcaster also fails local production in this way, then the situation in indeed bleak.

However, *Our Boys* has sustained its interest down to the 1990s for other reasons as well. The film is a remembrance of, and an exploration of, a Christian Brothers' education of the 1950s, written autobiographically by Black himself in collaboration with Dermot Healy. As with many of the films of this period, *Our Boys* employs a complex formal structure, mixing filmic discourses. Firstly, there is a fairly naturalistic fiction drama about a Christian Brothers school in Dublin at the turn of the 1950s/1960s. This drama involves two storylines – the beating of a young boy by one of the Brothers and the subsequent complaint from the parents and secondly the issues involved in closing down the school because of falling rolls and a changing social and educational environment. The second filmic discourse involves documentary interviews with former pupils of the Brothers and a contemporary interview with a Brother who assesses the educational legacy of the Brothers' style of education. These are direct address to camera interviews shot in conventional documentary style.

The third filmic discourse involves the use of archive footage and in particular two sequences which hold a deep significance for contemporary Ireland. The first archive sequence opens the film, with footage of a St Patrick's Day parade in Dublin, probably in the early 1960s. Floats in the parade include references to space exploration and the novelty of television and the footage captures the atmosphere in Ireland as it slowly came out of its long, protectionist period to embrace modernisation and liberalisation. This footage is used to establish the time and the locale of the film's dramatic sequences, but the period of change which it conjures up has a deep resonance in Irish culture, marking as it has done the beginning of a period of self-reflection and reassessment which, I would argue, has continued down to the 1990s. The second archive sequence is from the Eucharistic Congress, held in Dublin in 1932, showing the arrival of the papal nuncio in Dun Laoghaire. He is greeted by local and national politicians who approach, bow and kiss his ring, pledging their allegiance to the Church. The footage continues with scenes shot at the open air Mass in Phoenix Park which was attended by over one million people.

These sequences serve a double purpose. Firstly, they give a rather graphic illustration of how closely intertwined Irish civil authority and Catholic Church authority were in the period after independence. Indeed, as J.J. Lee points out, the Eucharistic Congress coincided with the election victory of de Valera's Fianna Fáil and Fianna Fáil played the Catholic card for all it was worth :

> De Valera would square the religious circle in the most electorally remunerative manner. In June, the Eucharistic Congress provided him with a timely opportunity to baptize his synthesis of republicanism and Catholicism, reminding the papal legate, in his feline way, that he was a loyal son of Rome.[27]

This archive sequence, in other words, provides the context for the film's exploration of Catholic education, itself a unique synthesis of religion and nationalism, and provides an earlier reference point against which the changes of the 1960s might be measured.

The second function of the Eucharistic Congress footage is much more contemporary and arguably much more significant. In September 1979, as Cathal Black was struggling to put his film together, Pope John Paul II made his historic visit to Ireland. He too received the political authorities before going on to celebrate Mass in Phoenix Park in front of more than one million people. The contemporary parallels were there to be drawn and the archive footage of the Eucharistic Congress does just that. Indeed, these contemporary resonances make *Our Boys* a peculiarly prescient film. What this footage raises is the question of just how much Ireland has in fact changed. In 1979/81, when he was cobbling together the budget for his film, Cathal Black was not to know that the Pope's visit to Ireland in 1979 was to be the catalyst in a conservative Catholic counter-attack against liberalisation which would dominate political debate in Ireland down to the 1990s.

These archive sequences set up a series of oppositions which were to be central to these political debates – liberalisation versus conservatism; Catholicism versus secularism; modernity versus anti-modernity; progress versus tradition. They speak therefore beyond their filmic setting to the wider debate about cultural identity in Ireland.

The documentary interviews in the film are powerful in themselves. The two former pupils describe in graphic language the sadism and sexual repression which went with a Christian Brothers education and the Brother interviewed impresses in his complacency. But, placed in the context of the film's fictional segments, these interviews prove devastating. The fictional sequences dramatise the brutality and humiliation which the Brothers visit on their young charges and it is difficult not to be repelled by the sight of powerfully built, grown men physically abusing the young boys. But for me, the sequences which dramatise the lessons themselves are among the finest achievements in contemporary Irish cinema.

In a series of brilliantly realised vignettes, the film perfectly captures the bizarre mix of religion, nationalism, brutality and learning which went into a strict Catholic education. Simplified history and complex theology mixes with Irish language teaching, patriotic singing and ritual humiliation. Such is the power of these sequences that it is to Cathal Black's credit that the film manages also to elicit some sympathy for the Brothers in their social gatherings, in their dedication and genuine religiosity and finally in the sadness and regret with which they face their own uncertain future.

The church/state conflicts of the 1980s, which *Our Boys* so powerfully presaged, were fought around issues central to women. Two referenda in particular, in 1983 on abortion and in 1986 on divorce, raised the whole question of the influence of church teachings on the civil code. However, the issues involved were not merely those around threatened liberalisation, but they were central to the wider feminist debate over legislation and women's bodies. A series of traumatic events in Ireland, in the early to mid-1980s, focused these issues firmly within feminist discourse. The tribunal in Tralee over what became known as the Kerry Babies affair and the tragic death of pregnant teenager Ann Lovett in 1984, in particular, traumatised political/sexual discourse in Ireland in the years during which the referenda were held.[28] It is not surprising then, that these issues played an important part in the general debate about identity in Ireland, and increasingly became central to the discourse about modernity. Equally, it is hardly surprising that these issues should also feature prominently in indigenous film-making in the 1980s.

The best of these feminist films were produced in, and to a large extent, dealt with, the problems of Northern Ireland, bringing together the two discourses of gender and nationality in a productive tension.[29] Pat Murphy's *Maeve* (1981) and *Ann Devlin* (1984) are concerned specifically with the place of women within the predominantly male discourse of nationalism. *Maeve*, in particular, probes these issues in a complex formal structure, deeply influenced by the counter-cinema strategies of the 1970s avant-garde.[30]

The film, though, which encapsulates the whole debate in Ireland about gender, nationality and modernity is Margo Harkin's *Hush-a-Bye Baby* (1989) produced by Derry Film and Video, a Channel Four-funded workshop.[31] In the film a fifteen year old teenager from nationalist Derry becomes pregnant and then suffers the trauma, guilt and repression which this entails in the tight, traditional Catholic community in which she lives.

The strength of the film lies in the way in which it delineates the paradoxes and contradictions of gender and national identity in Northern Ireland and in its sometimes harrowing depiction of women's repression. Indeed, the film brings into play a nexus of issues relating to core/periphery influences, addressing local, national and universal concerns in quite complex ways.[32] In this way, I think the film illustrates very well the space which a national cinema inhabits in regard to a *particular* response to the *universal*. The feminist discourse itself is a discourse of modernity, which impinges on the national discourse with considerable critical impact. But as *Hush-a-Bye Baby* also clearly illustrates, this universal discourse is *particularised* in its engagement with national specifics and the culture which emerges is no mere hybrid. It is a challenging and enriching contribution to the universal itself.

The films I have discussed, in other words, constitute in embryo, a cinema of national questioning, an attempt to re-imagine Ireland in new ways beyond the narrow confines of traditional nationalism. It is a cinema of doubt and scepticism, of instability and flux, of ferment and change. These are not films of bland assertion (though many of the films are 'committed' in a political and social sense). Rather these are explorations of the many-layered and contradictory nature of identity, explorations at the interface of modernity and tradition, of the particular and the universal.

This interface is analogous to that space identified by Kenneth Frampton as 'critical regionalism', an *arrière-garde* which 'has the capacity to cultivate a resistant, identity-giving culture while at the same time having discreet recourse to universal technique . . .'[33] A national cinema, therefore, is a form of critical regionalism. It seems to me that no matter how interesting the products of the American, or British, film industries are when they deal with Ireland, the films which grow out of the crisis of identity in Ireland itself, this critical regionalism, is the kind of national cinema which needs to be supported.

There are, of course, many precedents for this kind of cinema. One might argue, indeed, that all the great national film movements in Europe have been forms of critical regionalism. The French *nouvelle vague* of the 1950s and 1960s is exemplary here. This renaissance in French film-making was inspired by and became a response to the considerable presence of Hollywood cinema in post-war France. It was a total film movement, one that encompassed film theory and criticism as well as film-making. The theoretical imperative was to locate the personal factor in the artistic process of film-making and, ironically, this personal stamp was first located in the supposedly impersonal studio products of Hollywood. In criticising what he dismissed as the 'cinéma du papa', François Truffaut struck out for the cinema of the *auteur*.[34] His own films, for example *Les Quatre Cents Coups* (1959) or *Jules et Jim* (1960), and those of Jean-Luc Godard, *A Bout de Souffle* (1959) or *Alphaville* (1965), are particular (personal and national) responses to Hollywood's universality. As such, they also probe the nature of identity itself and, ironically, contribute back to the universal a body of work which is now seen as quintessentially 'French'.

One can detect a similar thrust in the New German Cinema of the 1970s. Thomas Elsaesser quotes a pertinent remark by Wim Wenders:

> . . . asked why American music, comics and movies had been his 'life-savers' in adolescence, Wenders replied: 'Twenty years of political amnesia had left a hole: we covered it with chewing gum and Polaroids.'[35]

Elsaesser argues that the New German Cinema pushed through this amnesia and by the time it had achieved considerable international success it 'appeared set to have its identity firmly located in a brooding obsession with Germany's own unredeemed and irredeemable past as a nation'.[36] These two movements are, of course, interlinked. While Elsaesser is surely right to locate this brooding, in psychoanalytic terms, in the loss of a father figure (a generation's loss of the positive identifications which the previous Nazi generation could not provide) nonetheless the catalyst for this identity crisis is the presence of American culture. Thus Wender's work, and that of Fassbinder, continually echo, reference and critique the 'American friend' in German national psyche.

It might also be noted that this kind of national cinema, the cinema of identity crisis, is not only a European experience. In fact, the same drives are present in recent Australian and New Zealand cinema and Dermody and Jacka draw on Elsaesser's analysis of New German Cinema to argue that Australian film is caught in two double-binds:

> ... it is caught in one double bind in asserting and also withdrawing from an identity that can never be taken for granted while it remains in accommodating dependence. It is also caught in another double bind, asserting and withdrawing from a sufficient 'difference' from Hollywood. These double binds became, effectively, the social imaginary of our cinema: it is a social imaginary caught out by the very problem of what might take place in its own space, because that cinema is attempting to project a national identity of such uncertain and self-conscious status.[37]

This formulation echoes the paradoxes of Irish cinematic experience which I have outlined above. What the experience of France, Germany and Australia demonstrates is that the particular problems in Ireland are regional and national inflections of problems that exist elsewhere. This, of course, confirms Espinosa's point, that the debate about cultural identity is no longer confined to the Third World. My argument is that in terms of film culture, and especially the desire for a national cinema, this transglobal problem never was confined to the Third World. The hegemony which Hollywood established after World War I effectively changed the relationship of national cinemas to their 'others'. The universal paradigm became Hollywood cinema and its presence in the culture of so many diverse national imaginings became the catalyst in the emergence, or re-emergence, of a recognisably national cinema.

The Irish experience, as well as the experiences and histories of so many rich and diverse national cinemas throughout the world, point to the future for film-making in Europe. The key is diversity. European audio-visual policies should be geared towards establishing, promoting and supporting a variety of regional and national cinemas within Europe's cultural boundaries. It should not attempt the impossible task of trying to compete with, or to replace, the universal paradigm of Hollywood.

Hollywood is so rich and so powerful because it can and does tap into the rest of the world for its cultural references as well as its personnel. It is the core culture which needs to attract the richness of the peripheries to maintain its cultural hegemony. Thus, as Kevin Rockett elsewhere in this volume has suggested, one can detect in the short films of many of the graduate students in Ireland in recent years, an attempt to master this universal film language. No doubt many of these young people will eventually move into the core culture itself, bringing their *specific* cultural experiences to bear on the universal form.

However, despite the seeming distance between the breakthrough films in Ireland of the 1970s and early 1980s and the recent upsurge of new, short film-making, the signs of this critical regionalism are still there. Thus in films as diverse as John Lawlor's *Sunday* (1988), Kevin Liddy's *Horse* (1992) and especially Orla Walsh's *The Visit* (1993) and Stephen Burke's *After '68* (1993), the spirit of critical regionalism is very much in evidence.

This spirit of critical self-reflectiveness is the constant element in all great film movements and national cinemas over the years. The national and transnational film policies of the European Union should aim therefore to nourish and promote this spirit, and ensure that specific, critically engaged film cultures continue to flourish parallel to Hollywood. If diversity of film cultures is allowed to wither and die under the inexorable advance of Hollywood, not only are many diverse cultures denied cinematic self-expression but, ironically, the universal paradigm itself will stagnate into the kind of monotonous global culture feared by many critics.

NOTES

1   An earlier and shorter version of this paper appeared as, 'Lear's Fool and Goya's Dilemma', in *Circa*, no. 50, March/April 1990.
2   Benedict Anderson, *Imagined Communities* (London: Verso, 1983).
3   Luis Buñuel, *My Last Breath* (London: Fontana, 1985).
4   Julio Garcia Espinosa, 'The double morality of cinema', *Vertigo*, no. 2, Summer/Autumn 1993, pp. 12-16.
5   ibid.
6   The best historical overview of the cinema in Ireland is Kevin Rockett, Luke Gibbons and John Hill, *Cinema and Ireland* (London: Routledge, 1988).
7   Quoted in Terence Brown, *Ireland: A Social and Cultural History* (London: Fontana, 1981), p. 55.
8   For an overview of cultural nationalism, see Terence Brown, *Ireland*.
9   Kevin Rockett, Luke Gibbons, John Hill, *Cinema and Ireland*, pp. 38–46.
10 Quoted in Kevin Rockett, *Film and Ireland: A Chronicle* (Dublin: A Sense of Ireland Ltd, 1980) (brochure).
11 Quoted in Kevin Rockett, *Film and Ireland*.
12 Kevin Rockett, 'Aspects of the Los Angelesation of Ireland', *Irish Communications Review*, vol. 1, 1991, p. 20.
13 Geoffrey Nowell-Smith, 'But do we need it?', in Nick Roddick and Martin Auty (eds.), *British Cinema Now* (London: British Film Institute, 1985), pp. 151–152.
14 Duncan Webster, *Looka Yonder: The Imaginary America of Populist Culture* (London: Routledge, 1989).
15 Kevin Rockett, Luke Gibbons and John Hill, *Cinema and Ireland*, p. xi.
16 John Hill, 'Images of Violence', in Kevin Rockett, Luke Gibbons and John Hill, *Cinema and Ireland*, pp. 147–194.
17 Albert Memmi, *The Colonizer and the Colonized* (Boston: Beacon Press, 1965) (with an Introduction by Jean-Paul Sartre), p. 87. See also a new edition, (London: Earthscan, 1990) (with a new Introduction by Liam O'Dowd).
18 John Hill, 'Images of Violence'.
19 Roland Robertson, *Globalization: Social Theory and Global Culture* (London: Sage, 1992), pp. 97–114.
20 ibid., p. 102.
21 ibid., p. 100.
22 John Tomlinson, *Cultural Imperialism* (London: Pinter, 1991), p. 90.
23 Kevin Rockett gives an overview of recent Irish film-making in 'Breakthroughs', Chapter Five of *Cinema and Ireland*.
24 ibid., p. 137.
25 Bob Quinn, 'Television and Locality : Gaeltacht Community TV', *Programme of 11th International Festival of Film and Television in the Celtic Countries* (Gweedore: Ireland, 26 April 1990), p. 12.
26 Susan Dermody and Elizabeth Jacka, *The Screening of Australia: Anatomy of a Film Industry*, vol. 1 (Sydney: Currency Press, 1987), p. 20.
27 J. J. Lee, *Ireland 1912–1985* (Cambridge: Cambridge University Press, 1989), p. 177.
28 For a feminist discussion of the Kerry Babies case, see Nell McCafferty, *A Woman to Blame* (Dublin: Attic Press, 1985). The best sociological survey of the Irish Catholic Church, including the role it played in the two referenda

of the 1980s, is Tom Inglis, *Moral Monopoly: The Catholic Church in Modern Irish Society* (Dublin: Gill and Macmillan, 1987).

29 For contrasting discussions on gender and nationality see two pamphlets in the LIP series, Edna Longley, *From Cathleen to Anorexia: the Breakdown of Irelands* (Dublin: Attic Press, 1990) and Gerardine Meaney, *Sex and nation: Women in Irish Culture and Politics* (Dublin: Attic Press, 1991).

30 For fuller discussions of *Maeve, Ann Devlin* and the work of Pat Murphy generally, see Claire Johnston, 'Maeve', *Screen*, vol. 22, no. 4, 1981; Luke Gibbons, '"Lies that Tell the Truth" : *Maeve*, History and Irish Cinema', *The Crane Bag*, vol. 7, no. 2, 1983; Luke Gibbons, 'The Politics of Silence: *Ann Devlin*, Women and Irish Cinema', *Framework*, nos. 30–31, 1986.

31 For a discussion of the making and reception of the film by the film-maker herself, see Margo Harkin in Martin McLoone (ed.), *Culture, Identity and Broadcasting* (Belfast: Institute of Irish Studies, 1991) pp. 110–116.

32 I discuss *Hush-a-bye Baby* in more detail in Martin McLoone, 'Lear's Fool and Goya's Dilemma'.

33 Kenneth Frampton, 'Towards a Critical Regionalism: Six Points for an Architecture of Resistance', in Hal Foster (ed.), *Postmodern Culture* (London: Pluto Press, 1985).

34 François Truffaut, 'A Certain Tendency of the French Cinema', *Cahiers du Cinéma*, no. 31, January 1954. Reprinted in Bill Nichols (ed.), *Movies and Methods* (London, University of California Press, 1976), pp. 224 –236.

35 Thomas Elsaessar, *New German Cinema* (London: BFI, 1988), p. 239.

36 ibid.

37 Susan Dermody and Elizabeth Jacka, *The Screening of Australia*, vol. 2, p. 25.

NOTES ON CONTRIBUTORS

John Hill is a senior lecturer in Media Studies at the University of Ulster.
Martin McLoone is a senior lecturer in Media Studies at the University of Ulster.
Paul Hainsworth is a senior lecturer in Politics at the University of Ulster.
Philip French is film critic of *The Observer*.
David Puttnam is a film producer.
Steve McIntyre is the chief executive of the London Film and Video Development Agency.
Colin McArthur is director of the Centre for Scottish Popular Culture.
Kevin Rockett is a lecturer in film at University College, Dublin.
Geraldine Wilkins is the acting director of the Northern Ireland Film Council.